Sultan Mehmed the Conqueror

GREAT EAGLE

Aytaç Özkan

NEW JERSEY • LONDON • FRANKFURT • CAIRO

BLUE DOME

Originally published in Turkish as *Fatih Sultan Mehmed: Büyük Kartal* in 2014

24 23 22 21   3 4 5 6

Published by Blue Dome Press
335 Clifton Avenue, Clifton
New Jersey 07011, USA

www.bluedomepress.com

Library of Congress Cataloging-in-Publication Data Available

ISBN: 978-1-935295-84-6

TABLE OF CONTENTS

To my wife and daughters,
who radiate my life...

INTRODUCTION:
THE TORCH PASSED FROM OSMAN
GHAZI TO FATIH (THE CONQUEROR)

The ancestors of Ottoman Empire, the Osmanoğulları (the sons of Osman) dynasty belonged to the Kayı tribe of Oghuz Turks. The Kayı tribe reached Anatolia from Asia during the reign of Seljuk Sultan Ala ad-Din Kayqubad bin Kaykaus (b. 1220–d. 1237) under the leadership of Ertuğrul Ghazi and they were settled around Söğüt and Domaniç in Bithynia region, the northern part of Anatolia, in return for their fine service for Seljuks. The same period also witnessed the severe oppression upon the people of Anatolia by the Ilkhanid Mongols, who started to rule over these lands after their victory in the Battle of Kösedağ (1243) over Seljuk Empire, and also distortions both in the economic and social structures of the society, which led to great chaos resulting with the migration of lots of Turkmen fleeing from Mongol tyranny into western parts of Anatolia.

In time, as the authority of Seljuks over Anatolia evanesced, Turkmen *beyliks* (principalities) governing the Aegean and Mediterranean coasts gained more power and independence. As for the Kayı tribe, upon the death of Ertuğrul Ghazi, Osman Bey was chosen as the new leader. Taking advantage of the crisis that the Eastern Roman (or the Byzantine) Empire was suffering, instead of challenging with those *beyliks*, Osman Bey, adopting a "ghazwa and jihad" (battle and striving) policy, turned his head towards the west, to Byzantine.

Since the very beginning, the Ottomans always preserved and sustained this policy, regarding it as the heritage of Islamic civilization and its political tradition until the breakdown. So within this context, the first period of the Ottoman state, including its establishment, flowed by seizing one by one the lands of those *takfurs* (Christian feudal landlords). Karacahisar, Yarhisar, İnegöl, and Bilecik (southern Marmara region) were among the provinces conquered first.

The *ghazwa* policy of Osman Bey, who was defined as "the most venturous and energetic leader" by contemporary Byzantine historian Pachymeres, was also supported by the notable and influential monde of the time. The Ahis, Ghazis, and some statesmen of Seljuks appreciated the strategies of Osman Bey and slowly gathered under his authority.

Osman Bey gained more prestige as he undertook the "leadership of ghazwa" among other tribes. He soon turned into almost an independent state of his own, especially after stamping money on his name (*tughra*, the signature of the Sultan). He continued *ghazwa* in Sakarya Plain, which unsettled the governors of Byzantine in the region and led to the breaking out of the Battle of Koyunhisar (Bafeus), also gaining the title as the first victory of Osman Bey in the books. Upon that, facing no obstacles or resistance, and as Pachymeres expressed, "*ghazis* (warriors) pushing the borders for ghazwa" now arrived at Bosporus's doors.

As for the social structures of Osman Bey's time, the members of Akhi order and *faqihs* (scholars of Islamic law) were valued both as the spiritual coaches of Osman Bey and also the organizers of judicial and social life. *Faqihs* were in charge of organizing the newly conquered lands and also the practice of Islamic rules. They served as the guides for their knowledge of Islamic law and tradition, and also worked as imams in provinces and villages.

In the year 1326, the hugest province of Byzantine in Anatolia, Bursa, was conquered and declared to be the capital by Orhan Ghazi. Troubled with the conquests of Turks throughout Kocaeli peninsula, the blockade they made at İznik and İzmit, and wanting to regain the lands he already lost, the Byzantine Emperor of that time, Andronicus III, ended up hardly escaping death in the Battle of Palekanon (1329), which had broken out as a consequence of these events. This was the first victory of the Ottomans over the army of the Byzantine Empire. Upon the victory, the conquests of İznik and İzmit also were accomplished, which completed the total conquest of Kocaeli peninsula. Along with annexing Karasids (1335), all southern shores of Marmara were controlled by the Ottomans. At the same time, attacking through the Dardanelle Strait, Suleiman Pasha, the son of Orhan Ghazi, seized Çimpe Castle (1353) and thus gained for the Ottomans the first land in Rumelia (the Balkans). Thanks to the capture of this castle, a base for expeditions to the Balkans was established and the path for the conquest of the Balkans was drawn. Sustaining *ghazwa* in the Balkans from then on, Suleiman Pasha also conquered some Byzantine provinces in Eastern Thrace in a very short time.

When we look at the reign of Murad I (1362–1389), son of Orhan Ghazi, we can see the outstanding progress in the Balkans. Conquering all the provinces in Eastern Thrace including Edirne, the Ottomans' enemies increased in number. Being irritated by this progress, and especially by the conquests of Edirne and Filibe, the Balkan states attacked the Ottomans within the first Crusade, consisting of Bulgarian, Serbian, Wallachian, and Bosnian soldiers, led by Hungarians. Ottoman vanguards sent on by Rumelia Governor Lala Shahin Pasha gave the Crusaders their first defeat in a sudden raid organized by Haji İlbey in the Battle of Sırp Sındığı (1364). The majority of the Crusaders trying to escape were drowned in the Maritsa River. After this victory, the Ottomans, wishing to accelerate the conquests, declared Edirne as the new capital. Also wishing to be a permanent fixture in the Balkan geography, they settled the Turkmen of Anatolia on these lands. Ottoman victories continued with Chernomen victory in 1371, forcing Bulgarian and Serbian kings to pay taxes to the Ottomans. A new Crusader gathering, which aimed to stop this puzzling and rapid progress of the Ottomans and expel them from Balkan lands, was once again severely defeated in Kosovo Plain. Walking around the battlefield afterwards, Murad Hüdavendigar was attacked by an injured Serbian soldier with a dagger, and died a martyr, becoming the first martyr Sultan of the Ottomans.

To sum up, throughout the reign of "Ghazi Hüdavendigar" Murad I, authority over Anatolia was strengthened, and Rumelia turned into the second homeland of Turks; in brief, the seeds of the Great Ottoman Empire were planted.

Succeeding to the throne upon the martyrdom of Murad Hüdavendigar, Bayezid I continued conquests in Balkan lands, too. In 1393 he annexed Bulgaria completely into Ottoman lands. He also achieved dominance not only in the southern Danube, but he also led his army in Wallachia and Moldova for the first time in Ottoman history, by crossing the northern side of the Danube. Along with the raids, the Morea Peninsula was pushed; however, even after being attacked four times during the reign of Bayezid I, the peninsula could not be won because of the luck and actions of the Byzantines. For example, in the siege in 1395, the Crusaders, led by the Pope, came to the Byzantine Empire's rescue. The largest group of the Crusaders created up to that time, including nearly all the European states, was trounced in the Battle of Nicopolis in 1396. It was such a severe defeat that forty-four years passed before the Crusaders were ready to re-attack. Thanks to the Nicopolis victory, all Balkan and European states had to recognize the authority of the Ottomans over the southern area of the Danube. The Ottomans maintained their settling policy, requiring migrations from Anatolia to Rumelia. Just like Seljuks once adopted Anatolia as a part of the homeland, now it was the Ottomans' turn to do the same to Rumelia.

With one hand continuing his conquests in Balkans, Bayezid I also annexed the Turkmen *beyliks* in Anatolia and expanded his territories to the Euphrates, turning into the most influential political agent in the region. However, establishing a strong Turk-Islam state in Asia, Timur regarded the expansion of the Ottomans along the Eastern Anatolia as a threat for his own presence. So, a battle, the Battle of Ankara, inevitably broke out between the two, with Timur emerging as the victor. This defeat had highly traumatic consequences for the Ottomans, for Timur did not want to leave a strong state behind as he was returning back to the capital of his empire, Samarkand, with the victory in his hands, and adopted a policy to divide the Ottomans into small principalities and have control over each. So, reestablishing the previous Turkmen *beyliks*, he also recognized the independence of each of the four sons of Bayezid I, leading the country into an interregnum that would last for eleven years. The throne wars of the four brothers, Suleiman, Musa, Isa, and Mehmed, was put to an end by Mehmed I Çelebi, who was dignified as "the second founder" of the Ottoman state for preventing the dissolution, and was thus deeply respected by the dynasty and historians.

From then on, Sultan Mehmed I made great efforts to regain the lands in Balkans and Rumelia, reestablish the state authority, and to re-provide the unity of the state. Meanwhile he had to deal with a set of domestic riots fueled by internal and external dynamics. As for foreign affairs, his navy, led by Çalı Bey, lost its first sea battle against Venice in 1416. However, he regained the control over the southern area of the Danube, and for the first time after a long period, sent his raiders (*akıncıs*) across the Danube. Dying at the age of thirty-two in 1421 from an illness, this skillful and energetic Sultan was attributed a special place in the history of Ottoman Empire. He saved the state from destruction, and united the nation.

Along with the enthronement of Murad II, while the other princes, encouraged by the Byzantines, were rioting, Anatolian beys also rebelled. After weary and long periods of effort, civil peace was achieved and a majority of Turkmen beys were annexed once again. However, the expansion of the Ottomans from Macedonia to Adriatic and Aegean coasts worried the Venetians. Moreover, Morea was also at stake. Inevitably, the Venetians and the Ottomans would not be any longer on the same page.

Sarajevo

It is understood that Murad II focused on the Balkans since 1430. Meanwhile, another Crusade, led by Hungarians and consisting of people from Serbia, Wallachia, and Bosnia, was defeated once again and right after that, as a result of the counterattack of Sultan Murad II, Smederevo Fortress fell, wiping the Serbian Kingdom out (1436). Although accomplishing that the principalities of Bosnia and Herzegovina pay taxes, Belgrade Castle, which was of vital importance, could not be won.

Upon the failure of the Ottomans before Belgrade Castle, making counterattacks, King Ladislaus I of Hungary and Ardeal voivode John Hunyadi expelled the Turks from Smederevo and ambushed Mezid Bey, one of the most famous Ottoman raiders. Supported by the Byzantine Empire, the Crusade, including the King of Hungary, Serbian despot, and Wallachian prince, entered into Ottoman lands by crossing the Danube and defeated Ottoman vanguards in 1443 in Niş Plain. Even Sultan Murad II could not stop the Crusaders. Even worse, after leaving the Ottoman Army, the head of Albania Beylik, İskender (Alexander), rioted at that very time. Intending to benefit from the crisis that the Ottomans were facing, Karamanids also attacked from Anatolia, which turned the situation into a more critical one. However, as winter descended, the Crusaders withdrew and a temporary period of ceasefire began, during which peace negotiations between the Crusaders and the Ottomans were commenced upon the demand of Sultan Murad II.

ON THE THRONE A LITTLE SON

On January 12, 1444, signing Peace of Szeged in Edirne, along with the envoys of the King of Hungary and the Serbian despot, Sultan Murad II moved to Anatolia to sign a peace agreement with the beys of Karamanids as well, upon appointing his little son Mehmed as the county governor. So, convinced that he secured both the eastern and western frontiers of the state, he addressed the statesmen that he summoned to his quarters in Mihalic Plain in Bursa: "So far up to this moment, I was your Sultan. From now on, my son shall be your Sultan, for I handed my name, my crown and my throne to him. I inform you all that my son Mehmed shall be your Sultan!" So he set out for his retreat in Bursa with dervishes and devotees after his declaration of abdicating his throne.

The sorrow he suffered from the sudden death of his elder son Ala ad-Din Çelebi and the burden of long and backbreaking challenges against the Crusaders played effectively in his decision. Besides, he wanted to introduce his son Mehmed as the legal ruler while he was still alive and give him some experience in terms of state affairs.

The state chronicler of the Ottomans narrated this very extraordinary event, a voluntary renunciation from the empery, with these words:

"... setting out from the effulgence of the sultanate for the wealth of poorness, and from the applause of ruling to the silence of retreat, he longed to reach eternal felicity. He opened his heart to his vizier Halil Pasha, saying; 'Listen Lala! For all this time our struggle has been for serving to God, for cleaning the weeds of Islamic countries and for chastening the enemies of both the state and religion. We spent our days for our religion. It is my desire to retreat for a while, to taste the loneliness and silence, only engaged with the *dhikr* (remembrance of God)."

AFTERWARDS THE RENEGED TREATY: VARNA

Succeeding to the throne after the abdication of his father Sultan Murad II, who had entrusted his son to the trustworthy and experienced statesmen, Mehmed II announced his sultanate through envoys to the heads of all great Islamic states, especially to the Mamluk Sultan.

A twelve-year-old child on the Ottoman throne after an experienced Sultan who had spent the majority of his lifetime in battlefields was regarded as an opportunity not to be missed. Besides the head of Karamanids, Mehmet Bey, was also provoking Christians to stand up by stating that "It would be taken for granted to wallop an inexperienced child as the present Sultan and that such bonanza would not hit once again." At the same time, both the Byzantine Empire and the Pope, disclaiming the Peace of Szeged, and expressing their conviction that it was time to expel the Ottomans from the Balkans, were pressuring the King of Hungary to annul the treaty. However, upon the assurance that he would be provided any kind of assistance just to take the revenge of the Nicopolis fiasco in 1396, King Ladislaus still did not want to break his oath, which brought Apostolic Cardinal Julien Cesarini from Hungary into play. Claiming that no agreement should be in force without the consent of the Pope, Cardinal Julien Cesarini annulled the Peace of Szeged, which had just been approved with the oath of the King of Hungary. To annul the treaties signed with the Ottomans and to lay siege to Orsova (a port city on the Danube) in early September were two oaths that were sworn on "Father-Son-Holy Spirit Mary" in the Royal Assembly. When Ardeal voivode John Hunyadi opposed the annulment, he was convinced when the kingdom of Bulgaria, which was meant to be retaken from Ottomans, was promised to him. Yet, John Hunyadi (also known as Johan Hunniad, Johan Hunyadi, or Janos Hunyadi) demanded more time for a declaration of war for as required by the Peace of Szeged, whose annulment the Ottomans did not yet know of, they would surrender the castles, and they did.

The rumors of the declaration of war against the Ottomans were very welcomed in Europe. This alliance included Bohemia, Wallachia, Croatia, Poland, German principalities, the Pope, the Republic of Venice, and the Hungarians. On the other hand, the rumors spreading that a new Crusade might gather became highly worrying for the Ottomans.

The new Crusade, led by the King Ladislaus of Hungary, reached Varna through Northern Bulgaria, crossing the Danube between the 18th and 22nd of September, 1444.

As a strong Venetian navy held the Gallipoli Strait, preventing access to the Balkans for Ottomans from Anatolia, restlessness and worry gave way to panic. Ottoman statesmen could produce no other solution than to enthrone Sultan Murad II once again. Receiving the news, he departed from Anatolia; however, he had to turn towards Bosporus, for the Dardanelle Strait had already been captured by Venice. The transition of the army to Rumelia through this passage cost a severe shelling by Byzantine galiots.

When the Crusaders reached Varna including Wallachia voivode Vlad Dracula, Sultan Murad had also arrived in Edirne with his army of forty thousand. Being informed of this arrival, the Crusaders were both shocked and distressed; to them, there was no chance for Ottoman soldiers to march in Rumelia since the Crusaders had occupied the Marmara and Dardanelle Straits. It seemed that once again, they were confronted with this brave commander Sultan Murad with whom they had fought against for years and years and it also felt like it would not be as easy as they expected.

On the other hand, the arrival of Sultan Murad II to Edirne caused both the people and statesmen of the country to rejoice. Meanwhile, summoning Lala Halil Pasha, Sultan Mehmed expressed his will: "Tell my father to stay here and guard Edirne from the heathens of Istanbul and let me go to fight against those Crusaders!" Halil Pasha responded: "My Sultan. I am not convinced to convey your will to your father, Sultan Murad. Thanks be to

God, he is now here with us. From now on he will be the leader, commander. It will be his word to be the order on us. Besides, this enemy is worse than worse. And you, my Sultan, are solely a fresh rose." Not satisfied, Sultan Mehmed turned towards his father himself this time and repeated his desire to participate in the war personally: "My Sultan! Please, I ask you to take me to this war. Let me be in there with my sword, fight against those heathens!" Yet, Sultan Murad II said: "No, son. Thou shall not. This enemy is hard. Thou shall stay here to guard this throne against Constantinople when I have reached the enemy." And then he headed out upon giving so much other advice to his son and was blessed with the prayers of his people.

Rapidly reaching Varna, Sultan Murad II immediately deployed his army. According to the plan, he would command the janissaries in the central line and Turhan Bey to the Rumelian soldiers in the right wing and Shahabaddin Pasha to the Anatolian soldiers in the left wing. Besides, Davut Bey was appointed to the left wing with the volunteers' army under his command. Upon summoning the notables, pashas, and his commanders in his quarters, Sultan Murad II addressed them: "You are my comrades in *ghazwa*. I want to witness the strikes of your swords upon those unbelievers. And thou know how high the martyrdom and *ghazwa* are on the layers of heaven. We all will be dead one day so we shall have a fine death, a martyrdom death. So let those killing the enemy be the *ghazi* and those killed to be martyrs then." Janissaries, beys, and pashas responded; "O Sultan! You have our word that we will sacrifice our lives to take the lives of those enemies of Islam, both for the love of you and love of our religion!" That night, Sultan Murad prostrated himself till the dawn prayer. When the morning arrived, the marches of the Ottomans towards the enemy began.

It was encouraging for the Crusaders that the war was during St. Martin's feast and they were outnumbered. King Ladislaus was telling his soldiers that: "Further away! Don't relax if they run away, go ahead and find them. Do your best! If we terminate Turks then there is nothing to stop us!" The Crusaders' army was of approximately one hundred thousand soldiers, while the Ottomans' was only sixty thousand.

A severe start of the war was given with the brave commander John Hunyadi at the left side of the Ottoman army and Vlad Dracula's army at the right side. After a while, cracks occurred in the determined resistance of Anatolian soldiers, while at the same time the Rumelian army was also withdrawing. Many heads of various beyliks, including Anatolian Beylerbeyi (governor) Karaca Pasha, lost their lives. Despite the cracks, Sultan Murad continued to control and commanded the war. Noticing that the war was going in their favor, King Ladislaus of Hungary attacked towards the center with Polish soldiers to reach the ultimate conclusion. The Ottomans did not turn down this act; yet, with their central forces opening and then gathering at once, they surrounded Ladislaus.

With a strike of an axe, King Ladislaus fell from his horse. His head, cut off by a Janissary named Koca Hızır, was placed upon a spear and erected right next to another spear upon which hanged the copy of the agreement that he violated. Comprehending that there was nothing more that could be done, John Hunyadi fled, accompanied by Hungarian, Polish, and Wallachian forces. The bodies of King Ladislaus and Cardinal Cesarini remained on the battlefield. While the Ottomans lost ten thousand soldiers, the losses of the Crusaders were much more severe.

As is customary with Turks, Sultan Murad walked around the battlefield after the war. He shared an observation with Azab Bey, a commander accompanying him: "How weird! A huge young man's army, having not a single old man!" "My Lord! Even one wise man would be enough to not dare to embark on such insanity. With the pride of their youth, they spoiled themselves," responded Azab Bey.

After the war, heralds were sent to Edirne, to all Muslim leaders. Twenty-five Hungarian soldiers, completely equipped and enslaved, were sent to the Mamluk Sultan. Upon being informed by the heralds of the victory, and meeting the chevaliers, Mamluk Sultan conveyed his benedictions for the Ottomans to the Sultan and cited the name of Sultan Murad in a Friday sermon.

As a result of this victory in Varna, the United Hungarian-Polish Kingdom, stretching from the Baltic to the Adriatic Sea, was given a huge strike. From then on, there remained no power threatening the existence of Muslims in the Balkans. Thus, the hope of the Byzantine Empire to get help from European countries was also terminated.

Turning back to Edirne from Varna, Sultan Murad did not hasten to go back to Anatolia; instead, he preferred to stay a while in Edirne to make sure that the danger was completely removed. No matter how much Halil Pasha and other statesmen insisted that he take the throne back, Sultan Murad retired to Manisa once again.

Soon after the departure of Sultan Murad II from Edirne, a competition began between the viziers of young Sultan Mehmed, Şahabeddin Pasha and Zağanos Pasha, and the vizier of Sultan Murad II, Halil Pasha. While the viziers of Sultan Mehmed were encouraging an active *ghazwa* policy, which attracted the Sultan, too, the others favored a more cautious and peaceful foreign policy. The "hawkish and dovish" statesmen were in conflict in the capital of the state.

In 1446, a huge fire occurred, causing suffering for many people and triggering the janissaries to rebel, stating that they wanted to have Sultan Murad II on the throne and threatening that if that were not so, they would enthrone Prince Orhan, who was residing in the Byzantine Empire. In addition to all this, some problems on the frontiers also emerged. Upon the persistent calling of Halil Pasha, Sultan Murad returned to Edirne and took the throne for the second time, while Mehmed was appointed to Manisa as *sanjak bey* (governor of the province), which brought peace, at least for the moment.

A Janissary soldier

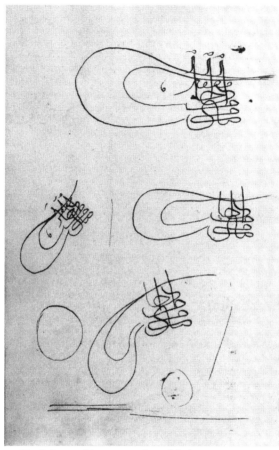

Fatih designed his own tughra while he was a prince.

His sultanate, lasting between 1444 and 1446, gained Mehmed much experience. He had the chance to better understand the state, the army, and the people, and also gained knowledge on foreign policy, and personally witnessed the delicate balances within the state. This first sultanate period had profound effects upon his character, too. His policies on breaking the authority of old and unnecessarily cautious viziers, bringing janissaries into line, and following an energetic *ghazwa* policy, and conquering Istanbul were all planted during these two years. And for his five years of service as *sanjak bey*, 'throne heir' Mehmed mostly focused on improving himself in political and cultural issues.

Back on the throne, Sultan Murad II focused on the Morean issue first. Soon after, the Morean despot who would also take the Byzantine throne, Constantine Palaiologos, took advantage of the situation after the battle of Varna and occupied land belonging to the Ottomans, and also rejected the demand of the Ottomans to withdraw his land seizure. However, left helpless upon the intervention of the Ottoman Army, Constantine had no other choice but to accept Ottoman authority once again. Then, the rebellious Albanian Bey, İskender, was targeted. The expedition also included young Mehmed. However, the siege had to be withdrawn since too many envoys reached the quarters of the Ottomans, stating that Hungarian commander John Hunyadi moved on again with his huge Crusader army to take his revenge of the defeat at Varna.

KOSOVO AGAIN TO EXPEL
TURKS FROM EUROPE

After the death of Hungarian King Ladislaus in the Battle of Varna, German Emperor Albert's young son, Ladislaus VI, was appointed as the new King of Hungary. John Hunyadi was assigned to guide the "child king." Benefiting from the naiveté of this brand new king, Hunyadi had the chance to act upon his will, even planning to take the throne by being the commander responsible for expelling Turks out of Europe. Hunyadi did not lose any time for his plans. Having been supported by the Pope and European states, he compiled a great army consisting of Hungarian, Italian, German, Polish, Czech, and Slavic soldiers—more than ninety thousand in all. He stepped on the Ottoman States with the seizure of an Ottoman land: Serbia.

Then, Sultan Murad reached Sofia from Albania and completed the preparations for war. Following the enemy, he stepped in the Kosovo Desert. The number of soldiers in both armies were nearly equal. As required by the Islamic tradition, Ottoman Sultan proposed peace in the first hand, however upon the rejection of his proposal, war was declared. On the army's central line, Sultan Murad and his son Mehmed were commanding Kapıkulu (Household troops) troops, on the right wing were Rumelian forces, and on the left wing, Anatolian soldiers. The expert raiders were assigned to be vanguards. The rest of the army was reinforced with ammunition.

The war in Kosovo Plain continued for three days, between October 17 and 20, 1448. Turks applied the wolf trap technique with mastery in the war. The technique was this: First the right and left wings gradually were expanded backwards, and thus the Crusaders thought that the Ottoman army was fleeing, so they attacked, which was expected by the Ottomans. The right and left wings then suddenly turned back and surrounded the Crusaders, leaving nowhere to run for the Crusaders. This action slowly beat them down and reached the target, devastating the majority of the Crusaders. John Hunyadi, the leader of the Crusaders' army, lost more than seventy thousand soldiers, and could only escape under the protection of firearms.

At the end of the 2nd Kosovo Victory, the facts that the Ottomans could not be removed from the Balkans and the existence of Islamic culture in Rumelia was permanent was clearly understood. Also the hope of the Byzantine Empire to get help from the Crusaders was eliminated. From then on, the Crusaders would be defenders, and the Ottomans, the attackers. Besides, the security of the western borders, which was essential for the conquest of Istanbul, was provided, thanks to that victory.

Turkish cemetery in Sofia

Afterwards, Sultan Murad II made an expedition in 1450 with his son Mehmed to conclude the Albanian matter, which he had left unfinished. However, because of abrasive attacks of İskender, rumors that John Hunyadi would make a move once again, and the beginning of winter, they had to turn back. That winter, for the marriage ceremony of Mehmed and Sitti Mükrime Hatun, the daughter of Dulkadir bey Suleiman, all friends and beys were invited to Edirne. Crown heir Mehmed turned back to Manisa with his wife after the wedding. On February

2, 1451, Sultan Murad unexpectedly passed away from a sudden stroke at the age of forty-seven. He was buried in Bursa Muradiye Mosque as required by his bequest.

Remembered as "Grand Murad Bey, Grand Ghazi Murad" for the deep love that his people had for him, Sultan Murad passed into history as a statesman, kind, gracious, fair, merciful, loyal, brave, cautious, and great leader. His *ghazwa* story, starting at the age of seventeen, continued to his last breath. He was a Sultan savoring conversations with scholars, preserving them, attributing his two days per week to scholarly meetings, and donating three thousand, five hundred coins to Medina and Mecca, and building poor houses for the needy in Mecca. Despite spending the majority of his life in battlefields, he also put importance on building many works, too. He was also remembered as "Ebu'l Hayrat" among his people.

SULTAN MURAD PASSED AWAY

Taking the letter of Halil Pasha announcing the death of Sultan Murad, Mehmed immediately reached Edirne and acceded to the throne on Thursday, February 18, 1451, as the seventh Ottoman sultan. He was nineteen. Byzantine historian Prince Dukas portrays that day as:

"All the beys were standing in line before him. A bit further were his father's viziers, Halil Pasha and Ishak Pasha. On the other hand, his own viziers, Şahabeddin Pasha and İbrahim Pasha, were right beside him as required by tradition. Mehmed turned and asked his vizier: 'Why do the viziers of my father stand that far? Tell Halil Pasha to stand closer, as is appropriate to his rank. And tell Ishak Pasha to go to Bursa for the burial ceremony along with the other beys. Besides, from now on he shall be in charge of issues relating Anatolia.' Then Halil Pasha and Ishak Pasha ran towards him and as tradition demanded, kissed his hand. Halil Pasha remained as vizier. Ishak dealt with the burial ceremony."

Mehmed appointed Ishak Pasha as Anatolian Bey and appointed Şahabeddin to his place. He kept Halil Pasha in the same position, despite previous conflicts, because he wanted to benefit from his experiments in foreign policy and also his skills. However with his new appointments and regulations, he left Halil Pasha all alone. Discharging Anatolia governor İsa Bey, son of Özgür, who was in charge of Mehmed during his years in Manisa, he appointed Ishak Pasha to his place. He also appointed Şahabeddin, Saruca, Zağanos, and İbrahim Pashas to the council.

The situation was a little bit different now: Owing to the Kosovo victory, the political condition of the state was amended, Ottoman authority in Balkans was reinforced, and Europeans were too demoralized for another Crusaders' army.

The representatives of European states, informed about the sultanate of Mehmed, came to the capital both for congratulations, proposing new agreements, and so on. Present were the envoys of the king of Hungary, the Mora despot, Wallachian and Genoan states, Lesbos and Khios Islands, Rhodes chivalries, and representatives of Genoan colonies in Edirne. Having forward-looking plans, this young sultan didn't turn down the proposals to have a peaceful foreign policy, for his main target was Constantinople.

The throne of the Byzantine Empire, which had only a few castles in the Marmara coasts and Constantinople, and which for more than a century and a half had been squeezed between the lands of the Ottoman state, expanding continuously, belonged to Mora despot Constantine XI Palaiologos since 1449.

In order to ensure the security of his borders, first Mehmed renewed the existing peace agreement with the Republic of Venice. Then he signed a new treaty with the Hungarians. He also treated Serbian envoys nicely, and thus some border castles were surrendered to him. In return for continuing to keep Orhan, grandson of Bayezid I in Constantinople, Çorlu Castle was surrendered to the Byzantine Empire and old agreements were renewed. Also, three hundred coins per year for the expenditures of Orhan were promised. However, this peace policy of the new sultan was misunderstood.

The return of Sultan Murad to the throne after the crisis in Sultan Mehmed's first sultanate caused Europeans to regard Mehmed as an incapable sultan. So, the death of Sultan Murad and the reign of Mehmed created a happy atmosphere in all of Europe. European kings were anticipating that the state would fall to pieces in the hands of that child.

Francisco Fielfo, who spent seven years in the Byzantine Palace, recommended taking action to benefit from this advantageous situation. In a letter to the French King Charles VII, he argued that the present Ottoman Sultan was highly incapable, a novice with no war experience, and that the Turks could only gather an army of at most sixty thousand. Thus, they would not able to resist, so the Crusaders could easily proceed to Constantinople, and working with the Byzantine army, they could easily expel the Turks from the Balkans, and could even defeat them in Asia and give them no chance to regain their strength. He ended the letter with these words: "So come on King Charles, move along!"

CONTINUOUS PROBLEM:
KARAMANIDS

The first attack against Mehmed II came from the Karamanids. Benefiting from the change in sultanate, the Karamanids occupied Ottoman lands. By sending the beys belonging to the Aydın, Menteşe, and Germiyanid dynasties to their former lands, he attempted to strike rebellion in Western Anatolia. These actions resulted in the decision of an expedition towards Karamanids. However, understanding that he had no chance before the Ottoman Army, İbrahim Bey had to seek peace.

During the expedition, surprisingly Byzantine envoys came to Ottoman quarters. Worried by this unexpected visit, the sultan had to accept the peace proposal of İbrahim Bey. Unsatisfied by the peace for he had the intention to dissolve this beylik completely, Sultan Mehmed had to agree to the proposal for he was afraid that the Byzantine Empire might do something disturbing. According to the treaty, Akşehir, Beyşehir, and Seydişehir would be surrendered to the Ottomans, and during an expedition, Karamanids would send reserves to the army. At the same time, the Byzantines, trying to make use of the occupations of the Sultan in Anatolia, were demanding new things using Orhan as their trump card. The envoys conveyed the message below to Halil Pasha:

"The Byzantine Roman emperor does not accept three hundred thousand coins as the annual payment. Because, just like Sultan Mehmed, as a member of Ottoman dynasty, Orhan has reached maturity. Every day, numerous people come to his door, addressing him as "Lord" and declaring him the ruler. Yet, even though Orhan desired to give them presents, he could not do this and always demands financial support from our emperor. However, there is no possibility of our emperor to meet all of his demands. That is why we have two demands: Either multiply the payment of Orhan or let us release Orhan. Because it is not our responsibility to feed a member of Ottoman dynasty. These expenditures should be met by the Ottoman treasury. If so, we will continue to keep him behind our walls."

As an ingenious diplomat and statesman and known for his meticulous and pro-peace foreign policy, for Halil Pasha it was highly unusual to respond in these words:

"You idiots! You silly Byzantine Romans! I know what you actually do plan! However, put aside your conspirations. Our deceased Sultan was a soft one. Yet, this new Sultan is not. You idiots. We still have the agreement including the oath of your emperor. Now you are attempting to violate it. We are not ignorant and weak babies. If you plan to do something, do it then! If you wish to declare

Orhan as the Sultan, do it then! If you plan to support Hungarians to pass the Danube, go ahead! If you yourself intend to attack and retake your lands, do not be late! But you shall know that none of these will be accomplished! On the contrary; what you have now will also be taken from you soon!"

Contrary to the overreaction of the pro-peace vizier, Sultan, having an active and pro-warrior foreign policy, responded with a weird tranquility to the envoys. Since Mehmed didn't want a rival that might ruin all his plans for the time being, he behaved very tolerantly to the envoys and said that he would be back to Edirne soon and that he might host them there later on.

Siege Preparations and the Last Efforts of the Byzantine Empire

Moving to Edirne upon solving the problem of the Karamanids, the young sultan reached Bosporus upon Kocaeli, for the Dardanelle strait was held by the European ships. While crossing the Bosporus, he said, "Lala, a fortress is necessary here," to Halil Pasha and gave the first sign of the Rumelian castle to be built right across the Anatolian fortress, made by Bayezid I. A new fort would enable him to keep the strait under control, enable easy crossings for Ottoman soldiers, and also bring limits to the acts of the Byzantines.

Even though the Ottomans ruled both the east and west sides of Bosporus, the strait that the Byzantines held was dividing the lands of the country into two. Not to have a total control over the strait was also putting the unity of the state at stake. If the conquest of Istanbul was the aim, then the strait had to be taken under control.

Upon returning to Edirne, Sultan Mehmed commenced preparations for a fortress. Feeling the oncoming disaster, the Byzantine emperor sent new envoys to Edirne at once. This time the agenda was not about Orhan, but rather, the envoys were trying to persuade the sultan to stop the construction.

"It has been a century since the Turks got Edirne. Since then, we have signed treaties with all the sultans. None of them has ever thought of constructing a fortress right next to Constantinople. When your grandfather Bayezid intended to construct a fortress in the Anatolian side, he asked the permission of Emperor Manuel. And the emperor gave his consent. However, you are preventing the transmission of the Europeans to Black Sea when everything is all right between us, and trying to make our people die from hunger. You are taking precautions to cut the custom taxes. Give up on your attempts so we can be good friends with you, too just we were with your father."

Sultan Mehmed responded:

"I am not planning anything bad for your country. To take measures for the security of my lands does not mean the violation of the agreement between us. It is still in my mind that your emperor hampered the army of my father to pass Rumelia, with his alliance with Hungarians. When your ships blocked the straits, you ridiculed the worries of Muslims. My father decided on constructing a fortress on the Rumelian coast even at the time of the battle of Varna. Now I am realizing his plans. You have no right to prevent me from doing anything I like in my own country. The Anatolian coast is mine because its people are Muslims. Even the Rumelian coast is mine for you do not know how to protect it. Now turn back and tell your lord that the present Sultan of the Ottomans is not like the previous ones. Even their vision did not reach where my rule had."

After all the preparations were completed, Mehmed came to the region to commence and personally participate into the work of the fortress. As narrated by Kritovulos, he himself had chosen the construction zone, he had the narrowest part of the strait measured, detected the sizes and borders of the fortress, and dealt with all technical details personally. He assigned Halil, Saruca, Şahabeddin, and Zağanos Pashas to monitor the progress of the fortress. The construction of Rumelia fortress including as narrated nearly six thousand workers both volunteer and paid, was completed in as short as four months' time. When looking at the fortress, the towers seemed like the name of both our Prophet, peace and blessing be upon him, and also the Sultan, "Muhammad."

As the construction was concluded, Mehmed appointed Firuz Agha for the commandership of the fortress, placing four hundred janissaries under his command and providing him with ammunition. Some of the cannons placed in the fortress had the capacity of their bullets reaching across the coast. There were twenty gates opening to the sea and before every gate cannons were placed. Firuz Aga was ordered to demand the determined tax from every ship attempting to pass the strait, no matter to which nationality it belonged and, if not, scuttle the ships with shelling. From then on, every foreign ship passing through the strait had to seek permission.

On October 26, 1452, the scuttling of a Venetian ship upon its attempt to pass through the strait without permission became a warning to others. Of a very strategic importance, Bosporus was now under the control of the Ottomans. As Dursun Bey, a historian of Sultan Mehmed period stated, "Since the erection of Rumelia fortress, even birds had to ask before flying through Bosporus." This was the first big step that Sultan Mehmed took in order to reach his target. Thanks to the fortress, Sultan Mehmed was now only a few millimeters from Constantinople and had a perfect overhead vision of the city. He turned back to the capital, Edirne, on September 1, 1452, after completing his observations in the zone.

Throughout the preparations, what the Sultan gave most importance to was to produce the biggest cannons ever. Since he was aware of the destructive power of the artillery, it was especially important to him to increase these cannons both in number and size. Ottoman engineers Muslihiddin and Saruca Sekban and also Urban, Hungarian cannon master fleeing from Byzantine to Turks, were appointed as this duty. On the other hand, Sultan himself overtook the issues of designing shells and bullets and making ballistic calculations. To have passed a successful rehearsal in Edirne in terms of shooting the balls enhanced the conviction for the conquest. The shells that the cannons threw weighed approximately six hundred kilograms and they could reach one mile away. This unique gun was named "shahi." On February 1, 1453, the cannons were set out to be carried out of Edirne, including fourteen battery cannons designed to be used in the siege and three more huge cannons. In order to provide the security of the voyage and to seize the castles on the way, a rivalry troop consisting of ten thousand soldiers was sent beforehand. It had taken nearly two months to bring the artillery before the walls. For the grading of the roads in the route, and the construction of the planned bridges, fifty masters and two hundred workers were assigned, and thirty coaches and sixty buffaloes were used to pull the artillery.

A quotation from Byzantine historian Dukas to express the importance Sultan Mehmed II gave to the siege of İstanbul, including his plans lasting for days and nights, and his extreme enthusiasm and excitement:

"Sultan was restless. All the time, in his sleep or during the day, inside or outside his mind was always busy with the conquest. He had already lost sleep. Continuously he was working on a map of Istanbul. One night, he summoned Halil Pasha to his palace and said in excitement: 'I cannot get this out of my mind. I have no peace, cannot rest. You shall know, I expect your support!'"

According to Sultan Mehmed II, it was a must to annex Constantinople into the divided lands of Ottoman between Anatolia and the Balkans. The Byzantine Palace turned out to be the home of all kinds of plots against Muslims and Turks. Starting after the 1071 Manzikert Victory and aiming at Kudus, the Crusades, the continuous Crusader Alliances starting with the Ottomans reaching Rumelia were generally planned and organized within the walls of this palace. The emperor was constantly inciting Turkmen *beyliks* so that he could prevent unity in Anatolia, and by protecting Orhan, he was planning to drag the Ottomans into a domestic war. Only with the conquest of Constantinople, the lands of the state, separated into two yards, could be connected and the permanent residence of the Turks in the Balkans could be enabled. In leading their soldiers from Anatolia to the Balkans, there were great challenges meeting the Ottomans, too. A Crusaders' army might easily approach from the sea and attack the Ottomans from behind, attacking from Rumelia. İstanbul was also of extreme economic importance for she had been lying on both the land and sea trade routes. Thus, Sultan Mehmed willed to rule over these roads and to make the European countries dependent on his control in terms of their economic activities.

As narrated by Islamic scholars including Imam Bukhari, Imam Muslim, and Suyuti, Prophet Muhammad, peace and blessings be upon him, had statements such as: "In my community, those who fight for the city of Kaiser, the emperor will be forgiven." Or, "The Last Day will not arrive till the city of Kaiser is conquered and the *adhan* is called there." In such words, Prophet Muhammad, peace and blessing be upon him, heralded the conquest and also honored the conqueror and the soldiers also heralding them with Paradise. One day Prophet Muhammad, peace and blessing be upon him, turned to his Companions and said: "Have you ever heard about a city surrounded by the sea of one side and by the land of the other?" And the Companions responded: "O Messenger of God! Yes we have!" Then blessed Prophet continued: "The Last Day will not arrive until this city is conquered with the yearnings 'Allahu Akbar,' 'La ilaha illahu wallahu akbar' of seventy thousand *ghazis*." And here is given the saying of Prophet Muhammad, peace and blessings be upon him, which was most frequently remembered and referred to by the Ottomans: "Surely, Constantinople shall be conquered one day. How blessed the commander who will conquer it, and how blessed his army."

Just like in the period of Umayyads and Abbacies, these narrations acted effectively in the desire of Turks to conquer Istanbul, and they included a holy love to the expeditions made towards Istanbul, and strictly believed that victory was a holy promise on themselves. However, despite many trials, the city could not be reached.

In the summer of 1452, while engaged with the preparations of siege in Edirne, in a meeting in which Sultan Mehmed was addressing statesmen and commanders, he said: ". . . Unless Constantinople is conquered, the danger of the Byzantine Empire will continue. For this city is dividing our country into two, and unless it is held by the Byzantine Romans, the unity of our state will be at stake. If the Byzantine Romans leave the conservation of the city to stronger forces, that would be worse for us. Please do not think it is impossible by remembering the sieges of my father's and grandfather's time. For the city escaped from the siege of my father and Sultan Bayezid I thanks to the helps of Hungarians and also Timur attacking us from Asia. For the help of Italians, now they are suffering from sectarian conflict against the Byzantine Romans. On the other hand, we are highly superior to the enemy in terms of our money, guns, war machines, ships, and soldiers. Either we lay siege to the city and get the city through war or we will force them to surrender the city to us. Nothing can hold us back!" Then he asked the opinions of some viziers and statesmen; some agreed with him; yet, some were opposed.

According to the opponents led by Halil Pasha, İstanbul was too hard to conquer and in case of a failure, the future of the state would be at stake. Also there was the possibility that this conquest would stir Europeans up and lead to a new crusade. For Constantinople was not only economically and politically important, but also religiously important. So, any attempt against the Byzantine Empire might give birth to negative consequences like before. One of the historians of the time who was participating in the siege personally, Dursun Bey, stated that some of the influential statesmen objected against the young Sultan continuously thinking about İstanbul and that such an attempt would create heavier costs; however, they could not change Sultan's mind:

"He would always be talking about the conquest. Rushed to move on at once. However, some statesmen and those in their services mentioned the difficulty of this attempt. They reminded him that previous Sultans spent too much money and gathered too many soldiers, yet still couldn't accomplish this goal. They also stated that any attempt against the city had the possibility to result with too much harm. So they would try to hamper the Sultan from what he was planning; but, they could not."

Exhausting from these oppositions, Sultan said that: "If it is my destiny to conquer that city, even the towers and walls are iron, I would turn into flames and melt them!" and expressed his determination. Finally with the consent of the majority of opponents, too, the decision was made upon the conquest of Constantinople.

As the preparations continued ceaselessly, Ottoman raiders led by Turhan Bey and his sons took action in the fall of 1452 in Mora and pressured the Byzantine Emperor Constantine's brothers, Mora despot Dimitros and Thomas. Turhan Bey was assigned to threaten and impose pressure upon despots throughout the winter so that with the help of severe raider attacks, Mora despots would be debilitated and they would be unable to send help to the emperor when the time came.

Rumelian governor Dayı Karacabey, on the other hand, was assigned with the conquest of the last pieces of lands belonging to the Byzantine Empire around Istanbul. He seized Misivri and Ahyolu lying on the Black Sea coast and the town of Ayois Stefanos in the neighborhood of Silivri and Vize. Bigados surrendered. They accelerated their works in the Gallipoli shipbuilding yard. Some of the newly produced ships were covered with copper. The commandership of the Ottoman navy, consisting of one hundred and forty-seven warships, was put under the control of Suleiman Bey. This navy also included nearly twenty thousand soldiers.

The Byzantine chain of the Golden Horn during the Ottoman period

As the Ottomans were being prepared in all aspects, the Byzantine Romans were completely silent. There were high-level statesmen in the palace of the emperor leaking information to the Turks. The belief that the city would be conquered by Turks was gaining popularity

among the people day by day. There was a Justinian statue right before the Hagia Sophia, and the red ball in his
hand fell over in the fourteenth century, which was regarded as a sign that the empire would end in the hands of
Turks. The people used to believe that this statue was
protecting the city. The narration that this statue, sym-
bolizing the sovereignty of the whole world, was point-
ing at Anatolia, and Emperor Justinian had said that the
person who would end his life would be coming from
that direction, was spreading among the public. Another
oracle was stating that, "The city would fall in the time
of a Sultan named Constantine." All these rumors reflect-
ed clearly how broken the people of Constantinople were
in terms spirituality.

Emperor Constantine spent the whole winter in preparations. He fixed all the walls and dug trenches nearly
to twenty meters, filling them with the waters of The
Golden Horn and Marmara; turning the city almost into
an island. What the emperor trusted most was the walls;
worn out, yet for centuries successfully preserved the
city from any raids and all attempts to conquer. Since the
walls in the Golden Horn side was only one-layered and
not as strong as others, another line of defense was erected, and in order to prevent the access of Turk ships to
Golden Horn, a strong chain was drawn from Sirkeci to
Galata. Six months' worth of food was stored, and the
Roman people were trusted to defend Constantinople

since they would obviously not dare to lose their commercial benefits in the East.

Giustiniani from Genoa, the famous commander to lead the defense, arrived in the city on January 26, 1453, with huge war machines and seven hundred soldiers, which created a joyous atmosphere among the people. It was a fine relief to have Giustiniani, famous for his brevity and heroism, in the country. He had fixed the walls with two thousand workers on his command, placed catapults where appropriate, and especially focused on the walls facing the sea.

These three-layered walls lying from the Marmara to Eyüp coasts were highly challenging for those trying to pass them. Moreover, there were trenches twenty meters deep before the walls. These walls, having been mended thoroughly three years before, were shaped like triangles. Planning to stop the attacks coming via land, the emperor also took some measures for sea attacks. Old ships were connected to each other with thick chains and sunk to prevent the access of Turks. Also, six thousand Byzantine soldiers and nearly three thousand additional soldiers were assigned to defend the sea. In the defense of the city, Italian, Spanish, Cretan, French, Russian, Hungarian, and paid Turk soldiers would fight, as well as Byzantine soldiers. Moreover, the highly effective Byzantine fire called Grejuva (Greek fire) was prepared, too. In order to cope with economic problems, jewels in the churches were used.

Wishing to gain the support of Catholics against the Ottomans, and stir the Europeans up, the emperor agreed with the Pope on uniting Orthodox and Catholic churches on January 12, 1452, for he was aware that he alone would not be sufficient. Cardinal Isidoros came to Constantinople on September 12, 1452, declared the unity of Catholic and Orthodox churches in Hagia Sophia, and performed a religious ceremony in accordance with Roman traditions. However, gathering before the church during the ceremony, people protested this act. Orthodox people strictly objected to this decision and stopped visiting Hagia Sophia, which quickly turned this place into a deserted one. They still remembered how in 1204, the Romans raided Constantinople, and how badly treated they were by the Romans. Byzantine people did not accept to give up on their religion and surrender their souls to Catholics just as they did not accept to give in to Turks. The instability and uneasiness in the city was at the top. Grand Duke Lucas Notaras, rejecting the unity of churches, said, "instead of seeing cardinal hats in Constantinople we'd prefer to see Muslim turbans." And he was actually translating the hearts of the people. The emperor had already lost most of his influence over the public.

TO BE HERALDED . . .

Upon completing the preparations, Sultan Mehmed set out from Edirne on Friday, March 23, 1453, with his army, viziers, and scholars, and arrived in Topkapı where he would set his quarters up on April 5. Kapıkulu (household) soldiers were provided with weapons and the others were ordered to prepare for war for the next day.

It was planned to start the war on Friday, April 6, 1453. The Ottoman army consisted of nearly eighty thousand people including volunteers and they were placed at the appropriate locations under the instructions of Halil and Zağanos Pashas. All the city walls, from Ayvansaray to Yedikule, were completely besieged. The pavilion of the sultan was set in Maltepe right across from Topkapı and around this, a huge Kapıkulu army was placed. Here was where the walls were weakest. Gunners were set up right before the central line. Long iron guns, various war machines, catapults, and siege towers were all placed in this line. The Byzantine emperor had also set up his quarters in that region, too, and the protection was attributed to General Giustiniani.

Right after the Sultan set out from Edirne, the Ottoman navy set out from Gallipoli, led by Suleiman Bey, the chief admiral, and arrived at the zone as well. The duty of the navy was to blockade the surrounding walls and to prevent the help that might come from outside. Also, it would attempt to get into the Golden Horn when finding a chance. The navy consisted of twelve galiots, nearly seventy sailing ships, and twenty transport vessels. The allied navy consisting of Byzantine, Genoese, Venice, and soldiers of the Pope were already holding the entrance of the Golden Horn.

After Friday prayer was performed altogether on April 6, 1453, when the deployment of the armies ended, an envoy was sent to propose to the emperor to surrender the city to prevent a war and deaths, as required by the Islamic tradition. Trusting to the walls and the help from outside, the emperor rejected the proposal. However, he stated that he could pay taxes, surrender all the castles except for Constantinople, and give some prestige for the Turks; however, this was not found to be sufficient.

Upon reaching no agreement, people walking among the soldiers declared that the siege had officially started. Despite all the age and wear, the emperor and his soldiers would defend their country and pride bravely. At the beginning of the siege, they were defending outside the walls when the attack was being performed by volunteers; yet, upon the arrival of the army, they had to withdraw behind their walls.

On the sixth of April, with firing of the cannons, the war started. Deafeningly, balls were being thrown along with the catapults, and also the archers were continuously throwing their arrows, filling the sky over the heads of defenders. However, it was not possible to break holes in the walls to enable them to pass through, for the holes were immediately being repaired. There were two big obstacles confronting the Ottomans: The walls and the Greek fire weapon, preventing Turk soldiers from getting close to the walls. One solution to that problem was to dig pathways under the soil and place dynamite under the walls. However, since every time they attempted this a new obstacle arose, they could not reach their aims. Just like the war on the ground, under the soil was a huge challenge.

In the eleventh of April, twelve huge cannons were placed in the guards before Topkapı in groups of three. The artilleries were accompanied by guns. They were not only shaking the walls but also the spirituality of the people. As hearing the voices of the artillery and watching the walls breaking down, people were praying to God for mercy. This cannon fire implied an enormous attack.

While the walls were beaten by the cannon fire, the twelfth of April also witnessed the Ottoman navy, of a hundred and fifty, gathered in Beşiktaş coast and after a rapid maneuver turned towards Golden Horn, which created great panic. However, the aim of Suleiman Bey was to check the navy power of the Byzantines, who were hugely disappointed, for it seemed that this time it would all be different, since previously the attacks were generally coming from land; yet, this time there was a strong power by sea, too.

On the same day, something negative happened. The envoys of the Hungarian king came to the quarters and declared that the Smederevo Treaty was not valid anymore, for Hunyadi was no longer a regent of the king. Returning the treaty paper with the sultan's signature on it, they asked for the paper with their king's signature. However, Sultan Mehmed ignored the envoy's threatening words—implicating a new Crusaders' army—and was highly determined to finish what he had started. Despite the worries placed upon the hearts of the people, the siege continued.

Severe cannon fire was now shaking the walls and wearing them out more than ever. However, the defendants were constantly filling the holes with stones, barrels, and planks. It was obvious that after that severe cannon fire, the Turks would attack. Thus, Byzantine soldiers were creating new defense lines with barrels and sacks filled with soil. However, they all knew, including the emperor, the public, and the soldiers, that the situation was different and much graver than before. The city had never been pushed to that extent and the walls had never been that damaged. The scene before their eyes was contributing to their hopelessness.

On the seventeenth of April, the Turks introduced their new war machines. Siege towers reached the walls and filled the trenches. Preparing for the main attack, the soldiers made the first trial on the night of the eighteenth of April. Starting after midnight, the attack lasted till the first daylight. Benefiting from the darkness, Turks attacked loudly after getting so close to the walls, accompanied by drums and so on. These frightening voices were heard by the people in the city, too. Soldiers tried to climb the walls with the help of ropes and ladders; however, the defendants on top of the walls were doing really well. Ottoman soldiers were trying to pull the defendants down with hooked spears, aiming to break the defending line. While the defendants were being attacked by arrows and cannon fire, Ottoman soldiers were trying to climb up; however, hot oil and rocks falling onto them did not let them advance any further. Finally, the soldiers were ordered to withdraw. Giustiniani and his soldiers played an important role in the success of defenders in this first attack. And the failure in the first attack led the Turks to determine to fire more and more on the walls.

The aim of this attack was to measure the defending power of Byzantines. The walls were generally encoded in terms of which parts were strong and which were not. Now according to these new findings, new strategies needed to be determined. Upon analyzing the condition of the walls, Ottoman cannons were placed between Edirnekapı and Topkapı; however, the defending power of the Byzantines was high and they were determined to fight bravely till the end. On the same day the failed attack, the Ottomans conquered Büyükada, which served as a relieving factor for demoralized soldiers.

A Janissary soldier with a musket

Envoys coming from Gallipoli on the twentieth of April informed that Genoese ships, providing ammunition and food for the Byzantines, had entered from the Dardanelle strait. Rapidly reaching the shores with the help of a strong wind, these ships had to stop as the wind suddenly ceased. Then, the Sultan ordered the capture of the ships immediately, and if the ships did not surrender, to devastate them.

Ottoman galiots, led by Suleiman Bey, attacked the Genoese ships waiting at the shores of Zeytinburnu with a huge rumble. Genoese ships were surrounded by Ottoman galiots. With the arrows flying from the ships and the stones thrown from machines, the war and huge chaos started. Brave Ottoman soldiers were trying to burn down the enemy ships and so were endeavoring to catch on ropes. However, the enemies didn't give them the chance, by continuously throwing rocks at Ottoman soldiers. When Suleiman Bey's flagship's ram hit into the enemy ship, a chest-to-chest combat broke out. Ottoman soldiers were trying to burn down the Genoese ships or burn the sails with the flaming arrows they threw, cutting their ropes and breaking down the body of the ship with their axes. On the other hand, for those in the Genoese ships, they were filling the barrels with water and extinguishing the flames around them, attacking Ottoman soldiers trying to climb up to the ship with spears, arrows, and axes.

Even three hours after, the Ottoman navy couldn't reach a positive conclusion. Upon seeing that the war was turning against the Ottomans, Sultan Mehmed had a burning desire to intervene in the clash and rode his horse towards the sea as if "he desired to take back the superiority" and ordered around both Suleiman Bey and the navy, yet he could not change the outcome. The Ottoman navy could not stop the Genoese ships with high sails and were rapidly floating towards the shore with the help of sudden and strong wind. The chain protecting the entrance of the Golden Horn was withdrawn to enable them to enter. With the arrival of these aiding ships, people and soldiers were encouraged. Watching this three hours' long brave clash, the Byzantines and Romans celebrated their victories. Now an enormous joy ruled over the city, while this defeat on the sea was resulted with a bad despondency among the Ottoman soldiers.

Sultan Mehmed became very angry over the defeat. Even he wanted to execute Suleiman Bey whom he blamed of being cowardly and disabled. With the intervention of other statesmen, Suleiman Bey was not executed, yet he was relieved of his duty. Instead, Hamza Bey was appointed as chief admiral.

At the night of twentieth of April, the Ottoman war parliament was gathered to negotiate the peace offering of the Byzantine emperor intending to make use of this defeat of the Ottomans. Now, the conflict between pro-sieges and opponents was feverish. Also among soldiers, there were some separations; some were supporting and some were standing against the continuation of the siege. The failure of Suleiman Bey gave strength to the opponents. Ottoman sources recorded the events of those days:

"The people of the city started to talk about the brave soldiers. Also this event saddened Muslims. Opponents used this as evidence and tried to guide the Sultan to give up on the siege. In this, the majority of the statesmen agreed with Halil Pasha. However, Sultan Mehmed was still determined even only a handful of supporters. A few religious scholars, especially Aq Shams al-Din and Molla Ahmed Gurani and from the viziers, Zağanos Pasha, were giving their support to the Sultan. These were not contented with to have peace with those nonbelievers under the siege. The Sultan did too much to cause the city to fall and did not approve the peace."

Opponents were claiming that in case the siege was prolonged, a huge Crusaders' army might rise in Europe and that they should be contented with a gold tax of seventy thousand, while on the other hand Şahabeddin Pasha, Zağanos Pasha, Turhan Bey, and Aq Shams al-Din and Molla Gurani as scholars supported the sultan. Even Sultan Mehmed himself for a moment thought about turning back. However, after distressing hours and severe discussions, it was decided to reject the offering of the emperor and to continue the siege.

The letter sent by Aq Shams al-Din with the signature of "Hızır" (Khidr) on this very challenging night is of great importance and today exhibited in Topkapı Palace museum. Having no chance of being fabricated, this letter has the characteristic of being the only instrument of the conquest that we had today. Translating into modern Turkish by Professor Feridun Emecen, the letter states:

"This event happened because that crew, which brought hopelessness and sadness to the hearts. There were fine opportunities, but they were missed out upon. It all turned against us. One of them was the joy of those unbelievers and their being encouraged. The other thing is that you could not control the events finely enough. Besides, there are some beliefs that my prayers are not enough. Now it is not the time for losing and neglect. In such situations, one should search for the people responsible. And then the responsible ones should be punished severely. If this is not so, they would behave worse when the castles are attacked and the trenches are filled. As you know, most of them are not actual Muslims and do their duties unwillingly. There are really few to sacrifice their lives for the pleasure of God. They sacrifice themselves only for this world. Now what I ask for you is, show your authority and conduct your orders. Assign those with less mercy, ensure that they are doing their jobs feverishly. This is also fine with Islamic rules, too. God says, 'O Messenger! Fight against unbelievers! Be strict to them!' When I was alone, something strange happened. I randomly opened a page from the Qur'an and encountered this verse: 'God promised the endless flames of Hell to unbeliever women and men. This is enough for them. God cursed them. There is a continuous pain for them.' As I said before, those are not real Muslims and so regarded as unbeliever. So they will accompany those mentioned in the verse in flames. You have the word, and you have to work strictly and severely.

"Strive, not let these efforts end in shame and sadness. You should know that we will be successful in the end, with the help of God. In fact, everything belongs to God, coming from Him. However, we should work as much as we can. This is the path that our Messenger, peace and blessings be upon him, and his Companion followed. Again, I slept after I recited some verses of the Qur'an in a deep sorrow. Thanks to God, I have witnessed some heralding news and favors of His. I felt really relieved for I have not been honored with such thing for a long time. This letter is to tell you some words, to your great existence, and for the huge love, I had in my heart for you."

On the 21st of April, with the cannons placed in the northern sides of Galata, Genoese and Byzantine ships were shelled. Upon not reaching the intended yields, these artillery were recorded as the first howitzers in history. The shells of the newly designed artillery were hitting their targets, flying over houses in Galata. At the same time, land walls were severely attacked. It was so severe that no one could even put their heads up. Walls were breaking down and fumes were everywhere. Those historically indestructible walls were breaking down one by one. The people of the city were now expecting a comprehensive attack after these shells. The happiness and confidence from their victory on the sea was now leaving being replaced swiftly with worry and fear. Black fumes rising from guns and cannons were spreading through the sky. However, the expected attack did not come. Thus, the defenders had the chance to fix the walls right after the shell attack, fill in the blanks, and find new strategies for defense.

The new chief admiral Hamza Bey made a few attempts to pass over the chain in the Golden Horn. The aim of the Sultan with these severe attacks was to press upon the Galata Genoese and the city as a whole for his big project in mind. This was actually for confusing the Genoese, so that the Genoese would not be aware the path opened before the Galata walls.

The night of the 22nd of April, the young sultan realized his incredible project. The hills before Galata had been smoothed over with hard effort, and on the path stretching from Marmara to Golden Horn were placed rafters and round objects, and these objects were finely oiled, created a platform for ships. That night, first small, then big ships were moved onto the land, and the small navy consisting of seventy ships landed in the Golden Horn from Dolmabahçe and Kabataş. In the morning, waking to see Ottoman ships in the Golden Horn horrified the Byzantines. This surprising move by the Ottomans created panic and fear among them. The Ottoman soldiers were completely freed from depression, and their conviction to conquer was strengthened.

One of the biggest enemies of Sultan Mehmed and the Ottomans, who knew the Sultan personally, Byzantine historian Dukas narrated this event with these words:

"Such wonder has never been witnessed nor heard about before. Persian king Keyhüsrev built a bridge upon the sea and as if walking on the land, he crossed his soldiers through the bridge. This new Alexander and to me the most magnificent sultan of the time turned the land into the sea and moved his ships over the rocks instead of waves. So, this sultan passed over even Keyhüsrev. For Keyhüsrev managed to pass Dardanelle Strait; yet, he turned back as defeated and humiliated by Athens. On the other hand, Mehmed overpassed the sea just like the land and devastated Byzantine. He got the queen of the cities, Constantinople, shining like gold."

Expecting an attack by the navy landed at Golden Horn, the Byzantine emperor sent some of his defenders there, leaving the land walls weakened. Everyone was convinced that the city, surrounded completely, would fall soon, and hopes for salvation had run out. The response of the Sultan to the Emperor, wishing to make peace under any circumstances was that:

"It is not possible for me to turn back and leave. Either I will get the city, or the city will get me dead or alive. If the emperor wills to leave, I will leave Mora to him and sign a peace agreement with him, give another province to his brother there. But, if I get the city with war instead of peace, then I will execute him and all the other notables. And I present the rest of the people to my soldiers as slaves. The city alone will be enough to me, even deserted and empty."

Being afraid that Ottoman ships in the Golden Horn might attack with the rest of other ships waiting at the entrance of the Golden Horn, Byzantine and Roman admirals were closely observing everything meticulously. They decided to burn down the Ottoman ships in the Golden Horn. The operation was planned to begin on the 24th of April, yet when it was postponed to four days later as suggested by the Genoese, Sultan Mehmed was informed about this plan and took all the necessary precautions. On the 28th of April, the Venetian ships' attempt was successfully overcome. The shell hitting directly onto the ship of Jakomo Kuko, who was leading the attack, scuttled the ship, the captain, and all the crew. Approximately a hundred and fifty people drowned and lost their lives. Leonardo from Chios narrated the event with these words:

"As turning back, perplexed, our ships entered into the port. Some of the marines falling into the sea reached the shore, yet were captured by the enemy. Their villain sultan ordered their execution before our eyes. Seeing that, our soldiers lost their temper and slaughtered them on the walls before their friends. So, now the war turned into a more brutal war as a combination of hatred and cruelty."

Another attack did not come after this event. Gunfire was continuing from land, while at the same time, the Golden Horn walls were being attacked. Increasing since the first of May, the poverty, chaos, and black marketing wore the people out. Leonardo from Chios narrates those days:

"A few times, we witnessed that Byzantines, in horror, left their places of duty using their tiredness, or fields, or wine as excuses. Some were stating that their families needed them and some were complaining that they did not have money and had to leave to look for jobs. When I told them they endangered not only themselves but also the whole Christian world, they responded me that: 'How can I care for the army when my family calls for me?' Then the food was ordered to be allocated equally to stop people's fear of hunger more than the war and to keep them stable in their places of duty. However, it was too late. The emperor had already lost his authority. He did not punish or execute those did not obey the orders."

Hopelessness and tiredness was more and more widespread among the people, so that they were even interpreting natural phenomena badly. For example, on a day that a huge crowd filled the streets to pray to God collectively for the salvation of their cities, they dropped the portrait of the Virgin Mary down from their hands, which was regarded as the precursor to bad things. Then the same crowd was subjected to a severe rain, so powerful that floods were dragging people away, even hampering them from standing up. These phenomena were interpreted as the precursor of disaster. On another day, immense fog ruled over the city, dragging people into depression. From then on, they strictly believed that "God had already left Byzantine." Additionally, between the Venetians and the Genoese, arriving the city for help, there was much hostility. They were blaming each other for being treacherous and cowardly. Soon this tension overflowed to the streets. Constantine XI Palaiologos asked for the Romans to end this situation and stated that they had to be together to stand tall against the attacks. The Venetians and Genoese promised the emperor to support one another again.

Being informed about the spiritual and psychological situation of the people of Byzantine, Sultan Mehmed ordered a second big attack. On Friday, the seventh of the May, right after the dawn prayer, the attacks were made around Topkapı, Edirnekapı, and Mevlanakapı. The walls around St. Romanus defended by Giustiniani were worn out, and three holes were made in the walls. There were chest-to-chest clashes between Turk and Byzantine soldiers, and a Janissary named Murad got close to Giustiniani and succeeded in injuring him with his sword. Then a Byzantine soldier, jumping off the wall, cut Murad's leg with his axe, and saved the life of his commander. Meanwhile, Rumelian governor Ömer Bey suddenly participated in the war in the walls; yet, he was stopped by the defenders and killed with the sword of one of the defenders' commanders, Rangebes. However, the soldiers of Ömer Bey immediately attacked Rangebes and smashed him. Clashes continued through the night.

A Janissary soldier of the Kapıkulu corps

On the 12th of May, a new attack was commenced before the Byzantine Palace and it was so severe that the public was nearly sure that they were close to the end; the city was falling. The Turks finally accomplished getting into the city from the holes of the walls; however, since no backup could be provided for the time being, they were pushed back. The next morning, the Byzantines collected the bodies of Ottoman soldiers around the trenches and burned them.

Since the 16th of May, bloody tunnel and mine wars started. The Ottomans planned to dig tunnels through the city and so enter the soldiers into the city. However, Byzantine engineers discovered the mines, and by collapsing them one by one, they martyrized the Ottoman soldiers beneath. On May 21, the tunnels around Eğrikapı were also found and collapsed. Another aim of these tunnels was to get close to the walls and put dynamite there.

On May 18, the Turks tried something new; they set up a siege tower with a height nearly equal to the walls. In order to protect it from gunfire, the skeleton of the tower was covered with oxide. Movable, with wheels, and containing a ladder inside, the siege tower had windows for firing from inside the body. Barbaro admiringly narrates that the magnificent tower was only created in four hours, and that he had never seen something so mesmerizing before. The tower stands before today's Belgrade Gate. Archers and gunners inside were constantly assaulting the defenders. This huge mobile tower was not only for attacking, but also an enabling machine for soldiers to get close to the walls easily. The tower might also be used for digging tunnels and mines. Upon getting close to the walls, a mobile bridge is used to transport the soldiers. On the same night, with a collaborative work, including women, children, the elderly and also the emperor himself, the Byzantines emptied the trench filled by Turks and burned down this siege tower with their Greek fire. However, it was getting more and more difficult for them to fill the holes in the walls caused by the huge cannon fire of the Turks. Even though the Byzantines did their best, it was impossible for them to completely mend the destroyed parts. The city was running to its end.

As required by Islamic law, when a city or castle surrendered, people living there could not be enslaved and their properties could not be plundered. However, if conquered, then enslaving and plundering would be the legal rights of Muslim soldiers and would continue for three days. Because Sultan Mehmed could foresee that the city would fall soon, in order to prevent this plundering and devastation of a thousand years' capital of the Eastern Roman Empire, he sent envoys to the emperor. Kasım Bey, the envoy, was met with ceremony by Constantine XI Palaiologos. Kasım Bey told the last emperor that the Sultan was avoiding what was oncoming after the fall of the city and asked for him to surrender the city of his own will, and if so, he could take all his properties and leave the city, and additionally he would be assigned as the Mora despot. He also added that the people of the city might leave the city with their properties if they wished, or they might continue to live in peace in their homeland. However, the emperor and his statesmen rejected this proposal. The emperor told Kasım Bey that peace would only be possible if the siege was lifted, and if so, annual taxes would be regularly paid no matter how much they were, and that the surrendering of the city was not possible neither by himself nor any other, and concluded his words by saying: "We are ready to die."

From then on, the only thing to do was to capture the city with a last attack. With his rejection, the emperor actually agreed on every possible consequence including enslaving his people, plundering all the properties, and that no one would be allowed to leave the city without permission.

On the 26th of May, something demoralizing happened in the quarters. The Hungarian envoy committee threatened the Sultan that if he did not lift the siege, a new Crusaders' army would come. They also declared that a united and huge army was about to cross the Danube and also a united European navy was about to enter the straits. Really, at that time, a big Venice navy was present in the Aegean Sea. This news panicked the soldiers and once again strengthened the claims of their opponents. Led by Halil Pasha, the opponents were insistent that if the siege would not be lifted there was a great depression awaiting the state. Halil Pasha was remembering his previous experiences including Varna and Kosovo II Wars and was worrying that Christians might attack with a huge army once again. Zağanos, Aq Shams al-Din, and some others were claiming that Byzantine might not get any help, and if so it would not be so important, and that the city had to be pushed unless it fell. Also, soldiers were getting impatient and restless, for it had been so long time and the war wasn't over yet. However, the heralds of Aq Shams al-Din and his followers, that the conquest would be accomplished, were encouraging people and the statesmen. In the last war assembly, the decision was made to continue to the war whatever it cost. Comprehensive preparations started once again.

On the 27th of May, cannon fire resumed severely. The old walls of Byzantine could not resist any longer against these new, powerful, and modern shells. The holes were getting larger and defenders were no longer able to fill them. A few groups of Turk soldiers managed to get into the city, yet were taken out immediately. The emperor was advised to run away; however, he made an honorable decision and stayed in his country.

At the night of the 28th of May, there a ceremony was organized with the participation of the emperor in Hagia Sophia, which was regarded as one of the most important sanctuaries of Christianity. This was the last Orthodox ceremony in Hagia Sophia. At the same time, in Ottoman quarters, the assembly gathered for the last time. The sultan sermonized here very effectively. Then he promised that he would promote the soldiers who first reached the top of the walls and planted the Ottoman flag there, and that new lands would also be given to them.

At the night of the 28th of May, flames burned and the city was surrounded. It seemed like the city was in the middle of a ring of fire. The walls were exposed to strong lights. Dukas narrates that very last night:

"When night descended, he ordered to light all the tents and to make fires. After the lighting, they all said *Allahu Akbar* (God is the Greatest). Those lights both in land and sea were lightening all of Istanbul, Galata, all the ships, and even Üsküdar on the coast across, more than the sun. The surface of the sea was shining. And Byzantine thought that a fire had broken out in the Ottoman quarters and was praying for this fire to devastate them all."

In the middle of the night, Turkish soldiers in their quarters were completing their preparations, praying on sajdah and waiting for the last order to go ahead. They were getting more excited and impatient. Upon checking the preparations, Sultan Mehmed performed ablution and started to pray:

"My God! You are the All-Knowing! You are the only one and you do need nothing. You did create that which was not born. However, they claim the trinity, Father, Son, and Holy Spirit. They excluded your verse 'From then on a Prophet will arrive and his name will be Ahmed.' They became those in the Qur'an: 'You are in an obvious deviance.' My Lord! As a slave of you, my only wish is to fight against those unbelievers and to deserve your awards. The will is yours the power is yours the mercy is yours. Please give us strength, help us to fight against them."

Wearing his sword, Sultan got on his horse and ordered cannon fire to destroy the walls before the last attack. The silence ruling moments ago was now torn by the deafening voices of the cannons and the fumes were everywhere. Benefiting from that chaos, Turkish troops got closer to the walls. Meanwhile, Byzantine soldiers were positioned for defense and ready to clash with the Turks. The Janissary band was playing hard.

The war started with the attacks from every perspective of the city. The Turkish army was pushing at the walls and the city as a whole. Especially at the land walls, there was a severe conflict. Crossing the trenches, Turks were leaning ladders against the walls. No matter how bravely Byzantine soldiers fought, they did not measure up to the Turks. According to Dukas, "Byzantine soldiers were not as masterful as an ordinary Turkish soldier. Because Turks were raised for that aim and every one of them was a more skillful archer than Apollo. They all were Hercules, they all were capable of handling ten enemies all alone."

Zağanos Pasha's troops were pushing at the Golden Horn walls, and the navy, led by Hamza Bey, was pushing from the sea. Marines were landing and trying to climb up the walls. When reaching no conclusion from the attacks, made successively two times, in the small hours, a third attack was ordered. Clashes were most severe on the line between Topkapı and Edirenkapı. Ottoman soldiers were trying to get inside the holes that were opened at that point. Emperor, Prince Theophilos Palaiologos, and Demetrios Kantekuzinos were trying to organize the defense behind the walls and encourage the soldiers. Arriving to that location, the sultan was also commanding his soldiers before the walls. As his last strategy, he put central troops and stand-by forces forward. It was certain that the final battle would be here. Seeing that the janissaries were going on attack, Giustiniani sent all his forces ahead. It was like doomsday. Janissaries were unceasingly climbing up the walls as if they were competing with each other with the sounds of *Allahu Akbar*.

Injured on his leg, arm, and chest, Giustiniani had no hope for victory. Even the emperor advised him to rest till the war ended, and he chose to run away by saying that, "he would be following the path opened by God for Turks," for he understood that it was impossible to turn the war to their advantage. Boarding his ship, Giustiniani set out for Chios. Realizing this, Sultan Mehmed led his last troops to the holes in the walls, too. The Ottomans were about to pass the most resisting walls of history and that capture the queen of all cities. The Eastern Roman Empire was kneeling down. Even though the last emperor continued to fight bravely and in tears, it was all ending.

Meanwhile in the Topkapı line, some janissaries succeeded in climbing the walls and remaining there. While Byzantines were trying to throw them down, the backup troops were preventing them. Finally, the flag of the Sultan was flying on the walls. Turks were, in groups, passing over the walls and entering into the city. And the last emperor whose soldiers were fleeing was still fighting in tears. Meanwhile he was felled with a strike of the sword and smashed beneath the feet of the flowing crowd. The flags of the Byzantine eagle and the Venice lion in the city were being ripped off one by one. Upon breaking all defensive lines, defenders started to flee and the people were gathered in the Hagia Sophia, and they continued doing so for months. However, according to Dukas, even at that very difficult time if an angel had appeared and asked them would they prefer to be Catholic and escape from Turks, or remain Orthodox but under the control of Turks, they would have chosen the latter.

Troops entering the city moved along the Hagia Sophia right behind the panicking and fleeing people. Winning the city with the war and conquest meant that for three days, plundering was free, and everyone knew that. Some of the public boarded the Venetian and Genoese ships, and breaking the chain in the Golden Horn, sailed through Marmara and met no blockage for the Ottoman navy had landed.

In the afternoon of May 29, 1453, the Ottoman army captured the whole of the city. The Roman Empire, which had ruled over the city for 2200 years, was now deleted from history. Sultan Mehmed was honored with the herald of Prophet Muhammad, peace and blessings be upon him, as in his saying, "Constantinople will be conquered. How wonderful is the conqueror and how wonderful are the soldiers."

Conquering Constantinople at the age of twenty-one and gaining the title "Conqueror," Sultan Mehmed entered from Topkapı to city with a huge ceremony, accompanied by statesmen, scholars, and commanders. The people of the city, in a panic, locked themselves inside Hagia Sophia. Dukas explained why people gathered there:

"According to the people's beliefs, when Turks entered the city, they could only proceed to the Great Constantine Statue, to Çemberlitaş. Here, an angel would give the holy sword of the empire to an ordinary person and he would chase Turks away from the city."

Breaking down the door of Hagia Sophia, the soldiers entering in did not attempt any massacre or oppression. In the Middle Ages, it was customary for an army to do massacres, when they conquered a castle or a city after a battle. However, the Turks did not want to put the blood of vulnerable people on their magnificent victory. Apart from those resisting, no one was hurt. However, plundering the city for three days, the soldiers got so many goods from looting that in the following years, a popular saying used for those who won fortune was, "Were you in Istanbul plundering?"

A Polish Janissary narrated: "Dismounting before the eyes of a patrician, clergy, and the public, Sultan Mehmed silenced the crowd who was sobbing on their knees and turned to the patrician and said: 'Stand up! I, Sultan Mehmed, address you and all your friends here that, from now on, do not be afraid of my rage, and do not fear for your life and safety.' Then he ordered his commanders not to treat the people badly, with a warning that those who did would be severely punished. He also assured people a safe arrival to their homes. Respecting the Hagia Sophia, Sultan Mehmed the Conqueror prevented personally a Janissary attempting to damage the sanctuary, and he opened his hand up to the sky and expressed his gratitude to God in these words: 'My Lord! My God! Thank you so much that you honored this slave of yours with the conquest of this city!' Then someone called the *adhan* upon his will. Turks listened to the *adhan* in peace. This was the moment that the Hagia Sophia was turned into a mosque."

On April 1, 1453, the first Friday prayer was performed in Hagia Sophia and the first sermon was delivered by Aq Shams al-Din, the spiritual conqueror of the city.

The future of the last Roman Emperor, Constantine XI Palaiologos, was not known for the time being, so a thorough inquiry was commenced to find the emperor, dead or alive. Some claimed that he had fled, while some claimed that he was hiding somewhere in the city. To reach a final conclusion, all bodies were taken stock of. When the head of the emperor was found by a Serbian soldier, the Byzantine Roman notables were asked for confirmation. When the head was confirmed to be the emperor's, Mehmed the Conqueror turned and said; "How fine God created you. Why did you waste yourself?" and the rest of the body of the emperor was detected from its clothing, for the eagle figurine as the symbol of the Byzantine Empire was dressed upon his purple boots, the color of the empire, and socks. Delivering the body to the notable Christians in the city, the Conqueror ordered them to bury the emperor in a royal ceremony.

After the conquest, Sultan Mehmed the Conqueror restored the Orthodox Church, which had already ceased to function, to represent its people once again, and appointed Patrician Gennadios as the head of the Istanbul Orthodox Church. He also gave the right to Jews to keep their synagogues. He also appointed Patrician Ovakim as the head of Armenian community and through these actions he accomplished a fine balance between all people.

Sultan Mehmed the Conqueror also invited Patrician Gennadios to his palace, and upon giving him a crown and staff, said, "Anytime you like, you can have my friendship. You have the rights and privileges of your followers." Then, with an appropriate ceremony, he accompanied him to the Church of the Holy Apostles, which was given to him as a residence. Here is a quotation from the communication Sultan Mehmed the Conqueror gave to the patrician: "No one shall ever oppress upon the Patrician. He and his priests shall be exempted from doing state services. The Byzantine Roman people shall continue to their customs and religious performances as they did before." From then on, it was given importance to keep the image of the patrician, and Palestine, Cyprus, Russian, and Balkan nations maintained their dependency on the Orthodox Patriarchate. The security of the patrician was also provided by a guard unit consisting of janissaries.

The main reason for this tolerance surely derived from the importance that Islam attached to the freedom of religion and conscience. History has witnessed that importance through the practices of primarily Prophet Muhammad, peace and blessings be upon him, and all the Islamic caliphs including the Rightly-Guided Caliphs. On the other hand, Sultan Mehmed the Conqueror might have planned to bind Eastern Christians to the authority of state through a patriarchate and in doing so, prevent a possible Roman Catholic influence over Byzantine Romans and other Balkan nations.

The long-lost tomb of the host of the Prophet, who was martyrized in the Istanbul siege in 669, in the period of Muawiyah, would be discovered with the help of the oracle of Aq Shams al-Din. When the tomb was opened, there was found a marble stone engraved in Hebrew that said "Tomb of Abu Ayyub." With the order of Sultan Mehmed the Conqueror, the graveyard mausoleum was built along with a mosque, madrasa, and a poorhouse. Martyrizing in the very first Istanbul siege of Muslims and keeping the flame of the conqueror alive for eight centu-

ries, waiting for the day to come, this honored companion would blow a sacred wind to the city from then on.

A muezzin, calling to Prayer

Some measures were taken to develop Istanbul, which has lost its population day by day since the invasions of the Crusader Romans in 1204, and the city was getting poorer and poorer. The Byzantine Romans, who left their homes during the siege, were assured of safe return. Also new Turkmens were brought from Anatolia and placed in different parts of the city. During the following years, as new areas were conquered, new artists and merchants were also placed in Istanbul. The first big mosque, Faith (Conquer) Mosque was built, which embodies a poorhouse, madrasa library, and so on. Hagia Sophia Madrasa was also opened and famous scholars and scientists in neighboring Turk-Islamic states were transferred there. For example, Ali Qushji, the famous mathematician and astronaut from Samarkand Madrasa, was brought to Istanbul and appointed as the head professor of Hagia Sophia Madrasa. The curriculum prepared by him was used in other madrasas, too. With the help of social and religious institutions also made by other statesmen, pashas, and viziers, Istanbul turned out to be one of the most important scientific and cultural centers of Islamic civilization.

With the conquest of Constantinople, eliminating the Eastern Roman Empire from history, but instead engraving the most magnificent victory of the Osmanoğlu dynasty, Sultan Mehmed the Conqueror declared the city as the capital. Now, the lands of the Ottoman State in Anatolia and the Balkans were united. Control of the straits, and the trade roads, including the Silk Road, was also given to the Ottomans, which meant the dependency of European countries economically on the Ottomans. However, this resulted in Europeans searching for new trade roads and so starting geographical explorations. On the other hand, as a result of the innovations in cannons, it was understood that no matter how strong the city walls were, they were not indestructible, which paved the way for breaking down feudalism and strengthening central kingdoms. It is also claimed that some Byzantine artists and scholars, going to Italy, pioneered the start of the Renaissance. So based on all these important developments, there have been some historians suggesting that the conquest of Istanbul ended the Middle Age and started the New Age.

BELGRADE:
THE HEART OF EUROPE

The title of Ottoman state as the "Ghazi State" was highlighted more than ever in the period of Sultan Mehmed the Conqueror. The fall of the capital of the Eastern Roman Empire and also the last castle of Christianity in the east was highly perplexing in Europe. Pope Nicolas V invited all Italian states to unite, and also called on Christians to unite under the same Crusader flag. Emperor Frederich III and the king of Napoli, Alphonso V, were very enthusiastic to lead this new attempt. In the emperor's assembly, gathered in Regensburg, the agenda was to have five years of peace among all Christian communities and to send a navy to the Dardanelle strait.

Being informed about the plans made against the Ottomans, Sultan Mehmed the Conqueror signed a treaty with the Republic of Venice, who might possibly be the leader of such an army, and agreed on the freedom of trade in the Ottoman state. The second aim of this act was to increase economical activities in the country. Securing the commercial profits in the east, Venice avoided participating in the preparations and plans for a Crusade against the Turks. On the other hand, after having signed a treaty with the Ottomans, Genoa forced their colonies in the Black Sea and the Aegean to sign treaties with the Sultan, too.

Sultan Mehmed the Conqueror determined his post-conquest strategy as to have a full control over the region up to the Danube, and terminate the Serbian problem. For he was aware that ruling over Serbia would be a great advantage over their strong rival in the west, the Hungarians.

In 1454 and 1455 two expeditions were made against the Serbian despot George Brankovic, who cooperated with the Hungarians and captured the front line castles in 1451 when Sultan Mehmed II was first introduced to the throne. The despot had to ask for peace, and with the ceasefire treaty, he agreed on to stop his cooperation with the Hungarians, and also to pay thirty thousand coins every year and to send a certain number of soldiers for the expenditures of the Ottomans. The efforts of Hungarians to spread Catholicism among Orthodox Serbians played an important role in the separation of Serbians from Hungarians.

Believing the necessity of the conquest of Belgrade to be permanent in Serbian lands, Sultan Mehmed the Conqueror set out for an expedition against Hungary in 1456 with approximately eighty thousand soldiers and a great number of cannons. Meanwhile, a small navy consisting of two hundred marines had already progressed towards Belgrade over the Danube. Belgrade Castle was established upon the junction of the Danube and River Sava, on steep ground that seemed like a peninsula. The towers and the body of the castle were highly reinforced, and the periphery was secured with trenches filled with water. Just like in the Istanbul siege, the Sultan brought some of his ships over by land and enabled those ships to access the River Sava, surrounding the castle. While the hopes of those in the castle were fading, it was announced that across the Danube a Hungarian army of sixty thousand led by John Hunyadi was on the way. Winning the sea warfare in the Danube, with a battle lasting nearly five hours, the Hungarian army reached Belgrade Castle, where a severe war broke out between the two sides. When the war turned against the Turks and John Hunyadi attacked right the Ottoman quarters, viziers suggested Sultan to withdraw, and the response was: "To give up on the enemy is the sign of a debacle. Thanks to God, I believe that God has the superiority and one cannot resist Him. It should be the enemy to run!" Then the Sultan, nearly unconscious, rode his horse against the enemy. As narrated by Ibn Kemal, while the Sultan was killing three soldiers with one strike of his sword, he was injured on his forehead and leg. Then the Ottoman army gathered strength and with the arrival of new backup raider force, Hungarians were pushed inside the castle. Heavily injured General John Hunyadi died soon after from his injuries. Gathering once again the night of this brave war, in the Ottoman War assembly, it was decided to retreat because of heavy losses, running out of ammunition, and the fact that the siege would definitely be prolonged.

This type of failure planted the seed of hope in the Crusaders in Europe once again. In 1457, sending its navy to the Aegean Sea, Pope Calixtus III sought an agreement with Uzun Hasan, the head of Ak Koyunlus and Georgians. Pope Pius II, known for his hostility towards Turks, and gaining the throne upon the death of Calixtus, called to the Christian states for a crusade.

Despite the worrying developments in the Christian world, still determined to terminate the Serbian issue completely, Sultan Mehmed brought the inheritance matter into the agenda upon the death of George Brankovic and his son Lazar successively. Hungarians willed the marriage of the daughter of deceased despot to the Catholic king of Bosnia, and in doing so, to take Serbia under the wings of Hungary. They also killed the brother of grand vizier Mahmut Pasha, Mihail Angelovich.

The Angelos family, including Mahmut Pasha, was one of two notable families in Serbia along with Kantakuzenos. Mahmut Pasha was a Devşirme at a very early age, and converted to Islam and before his sultanate, became a good friend to Sultan Mehmed. Upon conquering Istanbul, instead of Halil Pasha, Sultan appointed him first as Rumelia governor and then the grand vizier. Meanwhile, the brother of Mahmut Pasha, Mihail Angelovich, was promoted to the highest judiciary rank of

Serbia, became the head voivode. He was acting head of the Ottoman lobby in Serbia and struggling with the pro-Hungarian and pro-Pope factions. Unsettled by the pro-Hungarian and pro-Catholic policy of some notable Hungarians, the public seemed pro-Ottoman, and gathered around Mihail Angelovich. At the time Angelovich was imprisoned by Hungarians, the sultan assigned Mahmut Pasha with dealing with Serbian problem. Organizing two expeditions to Serbia in 1457 and 1458, Mahmut Pasha was challenged with this problem for two years.

The Grand Bazaar was a trust of Hagia Sophia.

On May 1, 1459, when Bosnia king Stephan married the daughter of the Serbian king, Bosnia was absorbed into the effective domain of Serbians and Hungarians. Some Serbian notables, rejecting a Catholic Bosnian kingdom, appealed to the Ottomans and proposed the delivery of Serbia. Upon this development, Sultan Mehmed the Conqueror made an expedition to Serbia and was welcomed by the public, and notably, he was delivered the keys of Smederevo Fortress. Then the Viseslav, Cernov, and Bala Stena Castles were also surrendered. Upon which, the whole conquest of Serbia was completed, and Smederevo was declared as a province and organized. Smederevo Fortress served as a base for raids towards Hungarians and the attacks from the West up to the conquest of Hungary in 1521 by Sultan Suleiman the Magnificent.

The fall of Smederevo was nearly as perplexing as the conquest of Istanbul for Europeans. Some found it a shame for the city to be surrendered without any defense, and yet, they did not want to see the real reason beneath this act. Escaping from the Pope and Hungarians, who were struggling to turn them Catholic by force, Serbian people preferred the Ottomans presenting them complete freedom of religion, and conscious of this, chose to protect their culture and identities. It is true that until 1877, when they were separated from the Ottomans and became an independent state with the Berlin Treaty, throughout four centuries they were never subjected to any kind of assimilation in terms of their religion or language, or any type of sectarianism.

THE END OF ISKENDER OF ALBANIA

Albania was captured in 1421 during the rule of Sultan Murad II. However, in 1443, during the Niş war with Hungarians, Iskender Bey, fleeing the Ottoman army and going to his country Albania, united Albania notables under the name of Lehza Unity and declared that he had rebelled to take the revenge of both his country and his family and chose a red flag dressed with a two-headed eagle as the symbol of his rebellion. Fully supported by both the king of Hungary and Napoli King, İskender Bey turned out to be a gun turned against the Ottomans.

Benefiting from the Ottomans' preoccupation first with the conquest of Constantinople, and then the Serbian matter, İskender increased his attacks against Turks in the region, which caused a response by Ottoman forces. Overcoming these forces, İskender Bey besieged Berat castle in 1455 with Napoli soldiers; however, he was beaten severely. However, once again moving on with the help of European countries' support, in 1457 he defeated Ottoman forces in Albulena Plain. With the help of this victory, his fame became widespread in Europe and he was awarded special entitlements by the Pope.

After a period of peace lasting to 1463, participating in the Christian coalition, İskender commenced his attacks again. Throughout this tiring period, the Ottomans had to fight against the republic of Venice, the kingdom of Hungary and Iskender in the west, and Ak Koyunlus and Kara Koyunlu in the east. Even though many expeditions were made against Albania, because of continuous wars both in the east and the west, they couldn't reach their targets. Finally with the capture of İşkodra castle, Albania became under the control of the Ottomans in 1479, and this situation lasted till 1912 until an independent Albanian state was established.

Right after the fall of Istanbul, the brothers of Constantine XI Palaiologos, ruling over Mora, Thomas and Dimitrios, had divided the land between themselves so one day they might rise as a problem claiming rights to these lands as the successors of East Roman Empire. Also, Mora was in a very strategically important location, lying between the Aegean and the Mediterranean and including important castles.

Despite Venice having included Mora in their own domain of effect, for conquering Byzantine, and claiming to be a heritor to the lands belonging to Emperor Constantine, Sultan Mehmed laid claim to Mora. In 1458, he made an expedition and returned to Edirne after conquering the northern side of the peninsula, including Teselya province, to his lands. Benefiting from the return of the

Ottoman navy, Thomas moved in on Mora once again with the support of Europeans.

Pope Pius II regarded Mora as the most important base for a possible attack towards the Ottomans, so he never wanted the Ottomans to have control over that region. However in 1460, Sultan Mehmed the Conqueror captured the whole of the peninsula except for a few places held by Venice. Thomas escaped to Italy and his brother Dimitros was bestowed the right to reside in Edirne after payment of sixty thousand coins.

Zağanos Pasha was appointed the governor of Mora. Annexed to Teselya, Mora turned into a province of Rumelia. Upon remaining under the control of the Ottomans until 1829, the region became an Independent Greek kingdom.

EAGLE IN THE BLACK SEA SKY

Established upon a small peninsula, Amasra was an important trade colony of the Genovese republic, not affected by the winds blowing from the east and west, with two ports and a unique beauty. The trade capacity of the ports was high. Moreover, Amasra was a city where illegal works were often being performed. The pirates in the Black Sea were plundering trade ships and taking shelter at the port, and the slaves escaping from Anatolia were hiding in Amasra for a few days then setting out to Rumelia from there with ships. In other words, here Genoese shippers were performing a kind of human trafficking and making huge profits.

Upon increasing complaints, the Sultan turned towards his grand vizier and asked why such an important castle was not besieged yet with these words: "Mahmut! Why was that fortress not sieged by my father and grandfathers?" His grand vizier responded: "My Sultan! I hope there is a fine reason for your answer and I hope God will reward you with the siege of this Castle." The Sultan continued: "Mahmut, you shall immediately start preparations for a siege. Let's see what God decides for us!"

In the summer of 1459, the Ottoman navy, consisting of a hundred and fifty, led by Mahmut Pasha, set out from Bosporus and sailed towards the Black Sea. Meanwhile, Sultan Mehmed set out by land with his army. It was a challenging path, passing through steep grounds and jungles, and when the Ottoman army arrived at Bolu, no one had any idea where they were heading. He responded to the question by saying: "If even one hair of my beard knew about my plans, I would throw it away." With this response, the sultan expressed the importance he gave to the confidentiality of state affairs and so he wanted to get to the enemy without giving them time to prepare.

İsfendiyaroğlu İsmail Bey, thinking that the Ottomans were coming for him, had left Kastamonu and shut himself up in Sinop. Perplexed by the siege of the Ottoman navy in the sea and the army in the lands, the Genoese realized that there was no benefit for them to resist and they surrendered the castle. Taking the city and making necessary regulations, the Sultan turned back to Bursa with a victory in hand.

Aiming to unify Anatolia, Sultan Mehmed the Conqueror was very uncomfortable because of the hostility of İsmail Bey in the area of Sinop. For he was attempting to cooperate with Karamanids, the enemy of the Ottomans and Christians.

Willing to end this little beylik, Sultan besieged Sinop Castle, both from sea and by land to reach his aim, without pouring any blood. Mahmut Pasha as an envoy said:

"Hey! Why don't you surrender the castle? How long will you resist? All of your provinces and ports are now controlled by our Sultan. Besides, your people recognize Kızıl Ahmed, whom we appointed as their Bey. From now on, get into the command of our Sultan if you wish to pass the rest of your life in peace." Then İsmail Bey, remembering his hostility in the past, said: "I am afraid that the Sultan will massacre me and my sons." Then Mahmud answered: "I don't think our Sultan would do that. He is merciful." And he convinced İsmail Bey to come and kiss the hand of Sultan Mehmed the Conqueror. Meeting him with respect, Sultan Mehmed said: "You are my respected brother. Please do not kiss my hand!" and hugged him. Then he was rewarded with control over Yenişehir, Yarhisar, and İnegöl.

Remaining as the Bey of Kastamonu for three months, his brother Kızıl Ahmed first migrated to Karamanid State, and then to Uzun Hasan. The Bey of Karamanids, inciting the old Kastamonu Bey İsmail, called him to rebel against the Ottomans together with himself: "Hey! Let's move on the Ottomans and call Uzun Hasan to attack from the other side. Let's end the existence of the Ottomans here, and you turn back to your own lands." However, İsmail Bey responded: "These words you speak are not fine as a Muslim. A ghazi Sultan is moving for *ghazwa*, to prevent him is not acceptable in Islam."

The new target of Sultan Mehmed the Conqueror was the emperor of Trebizond. When Constantinople was occupied by the Romans in the fourth Crusade number in 1204, the Angelos family established a state in the Mora and Laskaris dynasty in İznik, and the Komnenos dynasty in Trabzon. The Iznik king, expelling Roman Crusaders from Constantinople in 1261, revised the Byzantine emperor; however, the Komnenos dynasty continued to rule over the northeast of Anatolia, in Trabzon.

Trabzon

Right after the conquest, terminating the Mora despot, Sultan Mehmed the Conqueror was not satisfied with that and wished to wipe out the hopes for reviving the Byzantine Empire completely and end all kind of connections with the Byzantine Empire. Residing in Trabzon after the conquest, the Byzantine notables were regarding this empire as a hope to reestablish Byzantine. Just like the İznik king expelled Roman armies in 1261 from Constantinople and reestablished the East Roman Empire, they believed the Trabzon emperor would expel the Ottomans and reestablish Byzantine. That was why they were supporting any kind of action that would weaken the Ottomans.

So along with this reasoning, as a result of the expedition in 1456, Yuannis IV, the emperor Trebizond, agreed to pay three thousand golden coins in tax every year to the Ottomans. However, regarding the Ottomans as highly dangerous, the emperor sought cooperation against the Ottomans. Within this context, in 1458 he married his daughter to Uzun Hasan, the ruler of Ak Koyunlu state, and gave Cappadocia as a marriage dowry in return for protection in any kind of danger. However, he died when he was trying to include King of Georgia and Karamanids in the cooperation. The new emperor, Komnenos, communicating with the Pope, stated that he would undoubtedly participate in any expedition against the Ottomans. He tried to strengthen his navy and increase the number of his soldiers. Encouraged by the support of the Pope he declared that "he would not pay any more taxes to the Ottomans" and asked for backup from Uzun Hasan.

While the Ottoman army was in Sinop, the envoys of Uzun Hasan came to their quarters and demanded the exemption of the Trabzon emperor from taxes. He also demanded the payment of the taxes that the Ottomans had to pay them till then. The conqueror responded the envoys by saying: "Thou shall go to your home. Next year, I will come myself and pay my debt." Upon the arrival of Uzun Hasan and capturing of front line, the Ottoman navy, which people had thought would progress from the coast to Trabzon, surprisingly led to the south, Erzincan. Uzun Hasan remained helpless against this unexpected movement; he had no sufficient preparation for a battle with the Ottomans. He had planned that Sultan Mehmed the Conqueror would capture him in Trabzon, and that he would sneak behind and trap the Ottoman army in the steep zone. However, that was not the case. Upon his helplessness, he sent a committee of envoys, including his mother, Sara Hatun, for peace to the Sultan. His proposal was accepted on the grounds that he would not attack Ottoman lands and would not aid the Empire of Trebizond.

So, upon ruling out the best supporter of Emperor Komnenos, now the goal was to head for Trabzon. Since Sultan Mehmed the Conqueror did not trust Uzun Hasan once again, he kindly detained his mother Sara Hatun, as in these words he conveyed to her along with his envoys: "Mother! Your respectable son did not arrive, deprived of rewards of *ghazwa*. At least, thou honor us with your presence." Leading towards the north with his army, this was maybe one of the most challenging expeditions the Conqueror ever made. For, because of the lack of a straight and smooth path to follow, the Ottoman army had to proceed through steep rocks and mountainous terrain. As portrayed by Kemal Pashazada: "Not even a plain, even as large as a hand, nevertheless they surpassed the unreachable mountains, an army of clouds in the sky they became!"

For a brief moment, understanding how hard the Conqueror kept on moving, Sara Hatun asked: "O son! A Sultan like you, having such great beys at his door, should have been lying on feathers, so why? Is it worth for a castle?" Then the Conqueror responded: "O mother! Thou believed that this all for Trabzon Castle? The sword in our hands is the sword of Islam! These struggles of ours are for Islam. If we do not take any burden on this path, then wouldn't it be only a big lie to call it 'ghazi'? Even more we shoulder for God, for being honored by His rewards, is not enough!"

The navy, having already reached the castle, surrounded it through a firing ring. However, expecting backup from Ak Koyunlu, and foreseeing that he would be exposed to a siege from the land, David Komnenos was resisting. Yet, he was perplexed upon coming face to face with the Ottoman army. Seeing that they also had the mother of Uzun Hasan with them, he realized that from then that help from Ak Koyunlu would not be possible, and he agreed to surrender the city on the grounds that both the dynasty and the people of the city would not be harmed. Then he was sent to Serres, also providing revenue of three hundred *akçe* (silver coins) annually.

Topkapı Palace's Gate of Salutation, built by Fatih's order

Along with the conquests of Amasra in 1459 and Sinop and Trabzon in 1461, the Anatolian shores of the Black Sea were annexed to Ottoman country. Terminating the last pieces of the Byzantine Empire, the hopes of Europeans to revive the empire were completely melted.

QUAKING THE SKY:
CRUELTY IN WALLACHIA

No consent for cruelty, fairness we adore
Seek for the consent of God, His orders we follow
Avni

T he lands lying along the northern side of the Danube and mostly owned by the State of Romania today, was called Moldavia and Wallachia Principalities in the historical sources of the fifteenth century. These principalities survived, dependent on either the Polish or Hungarians. However, Wallachia principality had been paying taxes to the Ottomans since the period of Bayezid I, thanks to whom the Ottomans turned into an influential agent in Balkan zone. Moreover, the princes of these principalities were also being confined in Ottoman palaces as required by state traditions of the Ottomans.

This confinement practice was actually an ancient Central Asian tradition arising as a precaution to prevent the king from rebelling against the government. The confined princes used to be educated in the palace in the capital with the sons of Sultan and were raised with the characteristics of a leader to lead their own countries in the future. With this practice, the kings of the future would be shaped at very early ages, enabling their respect and fidelity to the state. However, the character analysis of these princes were meticulously made and when the time came, the most appropriate of them would be appointed as the king. This practice was also beneficial in terms of predicting the possible reactions of kings dependent on the Ottomans against some possible cases and developing policies and strategies accordingly or taking precautions.

Two sons of the Wallachian king, dependent on the Ottomans, Vlad and Radul, were sent to Edirne Palace, at the age of six and twelve, respectively. Being confined under the reign of Sultan Murad II, these two princes were educated with Sultan Mehmed from *lala*s (the tutors). Upon his father's death, Vlad was appointed as the prince of Wallachia in 1456 by Sultan Mehmed the Conqueror.

Vlad III, named as "Vlad the Impaler or Vlad Dracula" in Ottoman sources, *Tepesh* (hangman) by Vlachs and as Dracula (devil)" by Hungarians, had a very smart, energetic, and brave character, and through his abilities in leading and other skills, in a very short period of time he engraved his name in people's memories, defeated Moldova, and also gave a few defeats to Hungarians. Securing his seat in his own country and his increasing self-confidence soon turned him into a villain. Western books also attribute pages to his atrocities and tell about how he turned into a monster.

Ignoring his responsibilities towards the Ottomans, too in time, Vlad Dracula sought an alliance with Hungarians, and impaled Çakırcı Hamza Pasha and Yunus Bey, sent on as envoys after cutting off their hands and feet; yet, not remembering to 'respect' to the rank of Hamza Pasha, choosing a bigger stake for him! Right after that, he pillaged Northern Bulgaria with the Dobruja governor. In a letter he sent to Matthias Corvinus, the son of John Hunyadi, he boasted to have taken twenty-four thousand lives in his Bulgarian expedition.

Exhausted from the aggressive policy of Vlad, the people of Moldova were proposing an alliance with the Sultan. So, Sultan Mehmed the Conqueror made an expedition against Vlad Dracula in 1462. Avoiding a battle against the Ottomans, Vlad attempted something extremely crazy, sneaking into the quarters of Sultan at night to kill him. However, he managed to flee to Hungary upon causing too much damage. The king of Hungary, Matthias Corvinus, did not dare to spoil his relations with the Ottomans and imprisoned Vlad in his country. Then Sultan Mehmed the Conqueror declared Vlad's brother Radul as the king of Wallachia and annexed it to the lands of the Ottomans.

After a ten-year tranquil period, right after the sudden and accidental death of Radul, Vlad descended like a nightmare over Wallachia, whether by escaping from prison or being released. Yet, soon after, he was caught by Mihaloğlu raiders around Bucharest and executed. His head was exposed both as a sign of victory and to relieve the people. Turning into the nightmare in those times and providing a great source for horror movies today, Vlad Dracula was declared to be gone forever, unburdening the people of the country. So from then on, a stable and secure Ottoman period over Wallachia began, lasting until the 1877 Treaty of Berlin.

A Janissary sergeant

THE CONQUEST OF THE PEARL OF THE
BALKANS: BOSNIA-HERZEGOVINA

The art is to cultivate the city
The art is to cultivate the hearts in the city
Avni

Throughout the following years, Sultan Mehmed the Conqueror aimed both to continue his presence and progress in Rumelia and to capture the Dardanelle Strait and the islands near the Anatolian shores. Within this context, in his expeditions between 1454 and 1459, he annexed the Limnos, Lesbos, Imbros, Thasos, and Samothrace Islands. Thus the Ottoman sovereignty over the Aegean Sea was strengthened and the safety of the Anatolian coasts was provided. Considering that Lesbos Island is only twelve kilometers away from Anatolia, the necessity of the conquests of these islands can be better understood. The sultan also secured the capital with the constructions of Sultaniye Castle and Kilitbahir Castle across from each other in the narrowest parts of the Dardanelle Strait. Remembering Anatolian and Rumelian Castles that had already been erected, Istanbul had already been preserved on both sides.

The main objective of Sultan Mehmed the Conqueror was to unite all the countries in the south of Danube under his own control. Envisaging that a war between the Ottomans and the Republic of Venice would break out soon, the Sultan found it necessary to have Bosnia to press upon Venice by land. If the Bosnian principality remained an enemy to the Ottomans, that would bring about huge problems during the war. Unsettled by the conquest of Constantinople by the Ottomans in terms of his commercial activities, the Republic of Venice was also highly uncomfortable about the fact that Morea Peninsula was under Ottoman control. Aware of the developments, the principalities of Bosnia and Herzegovina demanded help from the Hungarians and Venice.

In 1458 when Serbian king Lazar died and Bosnian king Stephen Tomašević married his daughter, right after that, he put in a claim over the lands of Serbia and delayed paying his taxes to the Ottomans. He was also incited by the Pope, Venice, and the Hungarians and was promised support against the Ottomans. There prevailed a deep respect between the Bosnian people and Catholic royalty. So naturally, Catholic Hungarians and the Pope were supportive of the Bosnia king. However, the Bogomil people were resisting the oppressions and were keeping enmity in their hearts against the king. Since the peace, stability, and the safety of goods and people brought by the Turks to the countries they annexed was pretty well known, Bosnia was becoming more and more open to the Ottomans. Following the conquest of Istanbul, the Croatian king Stjepan Vukcic had already expressed his will within a letter signed as "Christian Voivode with the mercy of God and the Emperor Sultan Mehmed." Controlling all of Serbia, the Ottomans intended to break the Venetian and Hungarian effect on Central Europe by annexing Bosnia and Herzegovina.

In 1462 as Sultan Mehmed the Conqueror was moving towards the Wallachia voivode, he sent an envoy to the Bosnian king, demanding the payment of the delayed taxes. However, Stephen Tomašević showed him the treasury office and said: "As you can see, all the money is available here; yet I do not intend to send it to your Sultan. Because he seems determined to break out a war against me. I need all this money for a better defense and for myself to escape, just in case." And he imprisoned the envoy.

Hearing that the Ottoman army had stepped in Bosnia while they were returning from their expedition to Wallachia, Stephen Tomašević had no choice but to hide, for he couldn't get the expected help from Hungary and Venice. He escaped, and jumped from Jajce Castle to Srebrenik and to Komotin Castle; however, he finally gave in. Right after the conquest of Bosnia, Grand Vizier Mahmut Pasha was sent on to Herzegovina. The king of Herzegovina did not resist, so the country was conquered, yet leaving a small part to the king. The king sent his younger son to the Ottoman Palace, as required by the tradition. Converting to Islam, this little prince then was named as Hersekzade (Herzegovinian, the son of Herzegovina) Ahmed Pasha and was promoted to the office of vizier in time. Just like Serbia, Bosnia and Herzegovina were given the statute of *sanjak beylik* and annexed to Rumelia. Now the Ottoman country separated Venice and Hungary just like a wedge.

The king of Hungary moved to retake Bosnia from the Ottomans, yet Ali Bey Mihaloğlu chased the army away to Sava River and held many of them captive. The defeat of a great Hungarian army in the hands of a Turkish *sanjak bey* is significant. In 1471 and 1479, the king of Hungary reattempted to get Bosnia, yet had to turn back with defeat in hand.

Bosnians were of the Bogomil sect of Christianity emerging in Bulgaria. There were many points in which their beliefs differed from Catholics and Orthodoxies, and Bogomoils regarded their churches as the "sanctuaries of Satan." Contrary to the trinity, they believed that Isa was the prophet and a servant of God. They were accepting the Bible as the only holy source and rejected the opinions of the Christian church. They also rejected the clergy and its luxurious way of life, personal property, and consuming alcohol.

The tolerance that the Ottomans presented to Bosnian people in terms of performing their religious beliefs freely had profound effects upon the Bosnian people. Having already been exhausted from the efforts of Hungarians to convert them to Catholicism, Bosnians realized that this kindness of Turks spring from their beliefs, and just like Albanians, they converted into Islam of their own free will, without having oppressed to any kind of oppression.

Very pleased, when the Conqueror asked the Bosnian people if they had any demands or needs, they said that they also would love to serve in state affairs. And from then on they served fairly in army, palace, or other state affairs. The pact that the Conqueror gave to Bosnian priests reflects the approach of the Ottomans to religious functionaries and the value they give to the freedom of religion. Also, it lightens the background of Bosnians converting to Islam.

"I, Sultan Mehmet Khan, inform the world that the ones who possess this imperial edict, the Bosnian Franciscans, have got into my good graces, so I command:

"Let nobody bother or disturb those who are mentioned, nor their churches. Let them dwell in peace in my empire. And let those who have become refugees live and be safe. Let them return and let them settle down their monasteries without fear in all the countries of my empire.

"Neither my royal highness, nor my viziers or employees, nor my servants, nor any of the citizens of my empire, shall insult or disturb them. Let nobody attack, insult or endanger neither their life or their property or the property of their church. Even if they bring somebody from abroad into my country, they are allowed to do so.

"As I have graciously issued this imperial edict, I hereby take my great oath: In the Name of the Creator of the earth and the heavens, the one who feeds all creatures, and in the name of the seven Mustafas and our blessed Messenger (Muhammad, peace and blessings be upon him), and in the name of the sword I have, nobody shall do contrary to what has been written, as long as they are obedient and faithful to my command."

Turks named Muslim Bosnian-Herzegovinians as "Boşnak," (Bosnian). To this language, a dialect of Croatian, many words from Turkish, Arabic, and Persian were included. The Bosnian country remained under the control of the Ottomans until it was annexed to the Austro-Hungarian Empire in 1909.

THE GREAT BATTLE

An agreement was signed with the Republic of Venice, which was one of the most powerful countries of the Mediterranean, in the fifteenth century. Venice, which was struggling with its enemies in Europe, aimed to pursue a policy of peace with the Turks in order to protect its economic benefits in the east. And the sultan was aiming with this trade agreement to detain the powerful Republic of Venice from joining the Crusade expeditions, which were being formed against the Ottomans in Europe.

However, in the following years the Ottomans seized the areas that were permeated by Venice, like the Aegean and the Balkans, one by one, which led the republic to revise its policy. Venice was disturbed by Fatih, who started to hold the Aegean islands, and he invaded a big part of the Peloponnese, and finally seized Bosnia and Herzegovina, which forced Venice to search alliances against the Turks.

With the efforts of Pope Pius II, the Hungarians, who had the strongest land armies of Europe, the Albanian Skanderbeg, and the Republic of Venice, signed an alliance against the Ottomans. The spread of the Ottomans in the Balkans had limited the impact area of the Hungarians and repulsed them to the north of Tuna. Also, Skanderbeg desired to become the king of an independent Albania. The other states that supported the alliance were Lechia, Germany, Aragon, Castile, Naples, Cyprus, Rhodes, Ferrara, Modena, Savoie, Siena, Pisa, Lucca, Mantua, Trento, Genoese from Europe, and Ak Koyunlu, Karamanlides, and Georgia from Asia. The allies planned how to divide the Ottoman lands in case of winning the battle: Peloponnese, Attica, Thessaly, and Epirus was going to be given to Venice; Macedonia to Skanderbeg; Serbia, Bosnia, Wallachia, and Bulgaria to Hungary; and the Byzantine empire was going to be settled in Thrace, including Istanbul as its center. According to this plan, the Ottomans were going to be excluded from Europe. Uzun Hasan, the ruler of Ak Koyunlu, was going to take action from Anatolia in order to discard the Ottomans from Anatolia, which meant the Ottoman state was going to be exterminated.

The allies took action in the autumn of 1463, after Fatih came back from Bosnia. Venice attacked Mora, and Hungary attacked Bosnia. The Albanian Skanderbeg mutinied again. Simultaneously, the Venetian navy blockaded the Hellespont. So the great battle, which was going to last for sixteen years in the Balkans, the Aegean Sea, the islands, Peloponnese, and Anatolia had begun. On the other side, the papal edict of October 25, 1463, which commands the Crusade, was declared and read to public in Europe:

"You Germans don't help the Hungarians, so don't expect help from the French. And you French, if you don't help the Germans forget about the support of Spanish. You will be treated as you treat others. Emperors of Istanbul and Trabzon, kings of Bosnia and Serbia, and many other rulers taught us the end of those who watch the others vanishing. Sultan Mehmed, who obtained East Rome, is willing to obtain West Rome too."

A medallion with Fatih Sultan Mehmed's portrait

The Vatican also stipulated that every Christian who joined the Crusaders for six months would be forgiven from his sins. The money obtained from the papal edicts, which promised paradise, and the extreme taxes imposed because of the war with the Ottomans, was used by the cardinals against the Turks. But all the policies run by the Vatican, who was the central coordinator of the European states against the Ottomans, were observed carefully from Istanbul. The Ottoman spies, called *timar*s in some regions of Tuna, were very effective in Europe, working sensitively on this matter and delivering information to the capital city.

The first phase of the war, which started with the attack of the allies in 1463, ended with the victory of the Ottomans. In 1464 the Hungarians were excluded from Bosnia and the Venetians from Mora. The Balkan Orthodox were frosty about the crusades organized by the Catholics. According to Babinger the real reason of this frosty attitude was, "The hate of the Orthodox to the Catholics, was greater than the fear of the Ottoman occupation."

The Karamanlides proposed peace talks to Venice and Hungary in 1465 when problems arose; the army started to complain about the constant expeditions and the sultan had health concerns. But the sides couldn't agree each other's demands.

Although the Albanian Skanderbeg was invaded in 1466 it ended up with a repatriation to Istanbul without result. Albania continued to be a battlefront of the Great War with the Crusader Coalition till 1479. A military expedition was organized to the Karamanlides due to the growing menace in the Anatolian front.

THE OTTOMAN AGAINST THE
KARAMANLIDES-AK KOYUNLU ALLIANCE

Venice defeated its allies the Karamanlides and the Ak Koyunlu in Asia after being unable to get the expected support of the Hungarian king Matthias Corvinus. With the attack of the Karamanlides and the Ak Koyunlu from the Anatolian side a new front emerged in the battle.

After the death of İbrahim Bey, a fight for the throne started; Uzun Hasan, who had the support of Ak Koyunlu, became the ruler of the Karaman state. Thus, Uzun Hasan reduced the Ottoman domination in Central Anatolia. After Pir Ahmed, who took advantage of Uzun Hasan's death and acceded to the throne, demanded the return of some castles from the Ottomans, relying on Ak Koyunlu, Fatih decided to undertake an expedition to Anatolia. Fatih was relieved a bit after the death of Skanderbeg in Albania the same winter, and started peace talks with Venice and Hungary suggesting the possibility of concessions in order to distract them.

The sultan, who entered the land of Karaman in 1468, enthroned Shahzada (Prince) Mustafa in Konya after calling him from Manisa. With this move, he ventured a big struggle in Central Anatolia. Pir Ahmed took advantage of Fatih's return to Istanbul and the Eğriboz expedition, which started in 1470, and took back his territory with a counterattack. In 1471, the Ottomans attempted a comprehensive operation in order to take over the whole territory of the Karamanlides.

The plan of the alliance signed in 1471 by four messengers of Uzun Hasan with the Venetian doge against the Ottomans was: The Crusader's navy would supply support to the province of Karaman by the Mediterranean coast and the units of Uzun Hasan will come to the region and join them. The issue of Karaman became an international issue. Indeed a Crusader navy formed by Venice, Napoli, Rhodes, the Papal State, and Cyprus ships started terrorizing the Mediterranean coast in the summer of 1472. But Fatih directed Rumelian raiders to the region of Sivas regardless of the winter, and in the spring he walked on Erzincan with his great army, so he prevented the link of the Ak Koyunlu army with the Crusaders' army. It seemed that everything was up to the result of the war in Otlukbeli. The situation became extremely delicate for Fatih.

SULTAN MEHMED OR
UZUN HASAN?

U zun Hasan, who seized the capital Diyarbakır, and ended the throne fights in the year that the Ottomans invaded Istanbul, in a couple of years eliminated his competitors and transformed the Ak Koyunlu state to an empire with borders that extended from Khorasan in the west to the Euphrates river in the west, and from the Caucasus in north to the Arabian Sea in the south. He eliminated the Karakoyunlu state and transferred the capital from Diyarbakır to Tabriz. Uzun Hasan, who invaded countries and obtained success, considered himself as the greatest ruler of the region, and was annoyed by the victories of the Ottoman state, and he was saying: "The commanders of this region have seen my courage. If I had the opportunity I would show my daring and valor even to the Hüdavendigar." He even exposed his disturbance by not felicitating the invading of Istanbul, which was considered as a holy center of Christianity, and that act enraptured the whole Islamic world. The conquest of Istanbul wasn't even mentioned in the official history book of the Ak Koyunlu state. In the following years he took the rulers of Karaman, İsfendiyar, and

Germiyan, who lost their countries against Fatih, under his protection, he put himself in the place of Timur and acted as "The great ruler of the Anatolian seigniors." Uzun Hasan became more annoyed after the Ottomans eliminated the Empire of Trebizond and charged some additional tax for silk, which was the source of wealth of the Ak Koyunlu economy in Tokat. And because he was aware of the tension that was rising and the probable result of war, he accelerated his military's readiness. The aims of the alliance agreement that was signed by the messengers of Ak Koyunlu and the Venetian doge in 1471 was: Uzun Hasan will take Anatolia, the Ottoman sultan will be banned from constructing a castle in the coasts and would be forced to open the Black Sea to the Venetians. Peloponnese and the islands of Lesbos and Euboea would be returned to Venice.

After the Ottoman army began the Karaman expedition, Uzun Hasan sent an army of thirty thousand soldiers, formed by İsfendiyar, Karaman, and Ak Koyunlu forces to Central Anatolia in 1472. The units that arrived at the Ottoman borders sent messengers to Shahzada Bayezid, the provincial governor of Amasya, and Hamza Pasha, grand seigneur of Tokat, informing them they were aiming at Dulkadir, but then suddenly and fraudulently attacked Tokat. The city was looted terribly, and those who resisted were killed. Hodja Sadaddin Effendi explains this sudden raid as follows:

"They opened a hole in the heart of the land with terrible cruelty and brutality. They suddenly raided Karaman city, shredded the noble families of the city and drowned its people in oceans of chaos. They burned the houses of the city. They lowered people to such misery that they desired to sleep on soil and stones instead of bed and pillows. The books and documents that they set on fire burned like the souls of those who were burning from separation. Mosques and schools were set on fire and no sign of *minbar* nor *mihrab* was left."

Fatih, who was concerned about the advancement of Ak Koyunlu to Akşehir, ordered Shahzada Mustafa and Koca Davut Pasha, the governor of Anatolia, to be on alert. The Ottoman army that cornered the Ak Koyun forces, led by Mirza Yusuf around Beyşehir lake, obtained a decisive victory in the battle of Kıreli. "The Ak Koyunlu soldiers from the junior to senior, regardless their rank, didn't know in which direction to go. The majority were hit by arrows and some others were killed by the sword. And an incalculable amount of them were captured." The chief commander Mirza Yusuf was also among who were captured. Hodja Sadaddin Effendi gives some advice to the enemies of the Ottomans after describing the war, "Whoever draws a sword against the Ottomans, would plant the seed of trouble in the garden of his soul. You right-minded, if you want to be a *bey*, take your place in the shadow of those shahs. If you wish to have a pure life potion, don't draw the sword against them. God wished their empyreal, sharpened their sword in the path of religion. If you wish to find peace and respect, which is possible with wishing happiness to descendants of Osman."

An army of raiders of ten thousand soldiers was sent from Rumeli to Sivas, led by Mihaloğlu Ali Bey and his brother Iskender Bey, and crossed the path of Uzun Hasan, who was aiming to join the Crusaders' army that was waiting in the Mediterranean coast. Fatih was aiming for a pitched battle and a definite result against the Ak Koyunlu and their allies, and he spent the whole winter preparing for war in Istanbul. Meanwhile, a letter was sent from the Ak Koyun state to the capital city demanding to abandon Kapadokya and Trabzon. Also, Hasan and Timur were compared in the letter emphasizing how Hasan was greater than Timur. Besides that, the letter was reminding how Timur defeated Yıldırım Bayezid in the Battle of Ankara in 1402, like most of the rulers who took action from the East against the Ottoman state.

Fatih threatened Uzun Hasan and invited him to a pitched battle in response:

"Power and puissance are peculiar to Allah the Almighty. You escaped my rage before by your mother's request. And we have forgiven you, considering that you amended yourself and turned to righteousness. Although sovereignty for a cruel person like you in my time is illicit. Our allowance and tolerance led you to defeat some governors similar to you by violence, show pride and hauteur in your own land, even all your puissance and majesty is due to that. Yet you were entranced with your arrogance and forgot the sultanate law, we know well that you sent your soldiers to Tokat and the Karaman states that are under my judicious governance and oppressed the people, resorted to violence, and caused disgrace. We decided to take action this spring in order to punish you. Forgiving you is absolutely inconsiderable. Do not bother yourself. From now on our messenger is the arrow and our tongue is our sword. You think that demolishing a province is sultanate? We should bloody your chest for abusing our land without fear or hesitation. If you are brave come to the battlefield! Don't run away from a hole to another like a carven. Get ready, and don't say that we didn't warn you. Because your maligned existence shall vanish and excuse or apology is accepted."

In April 1473 the Ottoman army took action from Istanbul. Shahzada Cem was charged with the conservation of Rumelian land and was sent to Edirne as governor. With the joining of Karaman's flag officer Shahzada Mustafa and Amasya's flag officer Shahzada Bayezid to the army, the number of soldiers rose to approximately one hundred thousand. The Rumeli raiders were already protecting the ways around Sivas. Even though the grand vizier Mahmut Pasha offered after passing Sivas and reaching Şebinkarahisar: "My Great Sultan! Let's take Karahisar. Then we hope we find the enemy and beat him." The Sultan rejected his offer by saying, "O Mahmut! What should I do with the castle? I came to the enemy, find me my enemy!" and drew the attention of the soldiers to the real objective and showed stability in order to avoid losing time and energy.

Uzun Hasan's forces were first found around Euphrates Valley by chance in August 1473. It was narrated that Uzun Hasan, who was observing the Ottoman army, which was armed with firearms advancing in a perfect order, said "Wow, descendant of Osman! What an ocean!" The Ottoman and Ak Koyunlu armies proceeded along the edge of the Euphrates River pondering and trying to understand each other.

After the forces of Uzun Hasan retreated inwardly and disappeared, the Rumeli governor Has Murad Pasha, who was proceeding at the front, was raided after he crossed the river without informing the grand vizier Mahmut Pasha. The war between the Rumeli forces, formed by fifteen thousand persons and the Ak Koyunlu army of sixty thousand persons took three hours. The loss of the Rumeli forces, who were defeated, was approximately ten thousand. Except that some of the important statesmen like the conqueror of Mora Turhanoğlu Ömer Bey, Aydınoğlu Hacı Bey, the Rumeli treasurer Ahmed Çelebi were captured. Uzun Hasan's son Uğurlu Mehmed Bey, who defeated Has Murad Pasha, proposed to take action in order to reach the main Ottoman army, but couldn't convince his father of that. After darkness fell, the Ak Koyunlu forces disappeared. Signs of defeat occurred in the Ottoman army, and besides that a great anxiety dominated in Istanbul and Edirne. But Fatih Sultan Mehmed was able to elevate his soldiers as an astute leader and continued to search for Uzun Hasan with his soldiers.

According to Turhanoğlu Ömer Bey, Uzun Hasan laid entertainments for his soldiers and mocked Ömer Bey by telling him, "Ömer Bey! Did I cut the leg of the descendant of Osman? As the Rumeli soldiers were the honor and the only basis of the Ottoman army. I finished them and erased them from the book of existence. From now on the throne of Rumeli is mine and the palace is my residence." Ömer Bey responded to him:

"Master! Taking a drop from the ocean of the Ottoman army will not affect the sea from foaming. The wane of one star from the firmament will not affect its kingdom. Our sultan has a hundred thousand servants like me. The power, puissance, horses, and soldiers of our majesty are so many that taking a few of his slaves will not dust the mirror of his heart that is shining. How words can affect honor and pride. His fortune is a gift from Allah, state is his inborn essence. Those who be a rightful servant in his path, escape the trouble of time."

Uzun Hasan was inflamed and shouted, saying, "Look at this man, what he is saying while he is captured by us. What kind of nonsense his mouth is saying. He should be killed immediately!" in order to get out the hook Ömer Bey, who faced trouble, and said:

"The heart of the Grace Inn shouldn't be affected by my arrogant words. As the descendant of Osman has a great right on me. Forgetting their right is being a rebel. It is not right to talk about my benefactor. But the truth is that the soldiers of the sultan fell. And the rest were possessed by fear, were shredded, and lost their power to resist. They are not able to resist a strong attack."

After that Uzun Hasan said: "Lads! Ömer Bey is saying the truth. Forgetting the right of the benediction is infidelity and it is against the faith. Such a veteran and smart person."

The nerves were extremely strained in the Ottoman army, who couldn't get any news from the Ak Koyunlu army, and had to be careful about the possible raids. On Wednesday, August 11, 1473, the Ottoman army took a rest in Tercan Valley, which is surrounded by mountains and situated in a hard place to pass through, and they noticed the forces of Uzun Hasan in the ridge of Otlukbeli, positioned for war. In spite of the unpreparedness and the bad site where they were caught, the sultan accepted the war, because the army had enough provisions for only eight days. The seigneur of Anatolia, Koca Davut Pasha, immediately turned to the ridges in order to prevent the Ak Koyunlu army to pass through the ridges. When Davut Pasha attacked rapidly with thirty thousand Anatolian soldiers, the Ak Koyunlu units, led by Gavur Ishak, settled to the mountaintops, and consequently Ishak retreated. Also, the units of Kör Zeynel that attacked Davut Pasha on the platform of the ridge were stopped. The Ottoman army escaped a critical situation as the main Ak Koyunlu units stayed immobile, and they took their ammunition and proceeded through the ridges with the two armies in order to attack inside the valley.

A gravure of Fatih from a Western perspective

Shahzada Mustafa, who was commanding the left wing of the army, attacked Zeynel, the son of Uzun Hasan, as soon as he reached the platform. He moved Uzun

Hasan's units from the mountaintops almost like a flood. The two armies that were forcing each other inexorably, were opening and closing like the sea that drowned the pharaoh. Meanwhile, Shahzada Bayezid, who was commanding the right wing of the Ottoman army, attacked the left side of the Ak Koyunlu army. Uzun Hasan's other son, Uğurlu Mehmed Bey, was awaiting the chosen units and the central forces, which were under Fatih to join the war.

He was going to watch Kapıkulu soldiers enclosing him from his side and back and completely eliminating him. While the fight between Mustafa and Zeynel was ruthlessly continuing, Zeynel was captured after he felt from his horse and his head that was cut off was exposed in the square. With the heavy support of artillery and guns, Shahzada Bayezid defeated the left branch of the Ak Koyunlu, which was commanded by Mehmed Bakır, captured him and seized the flag of the army. Then Shahzada Bayezid turned to Uğurlu Mehmed's units, which were observing the central forces of the Ottomans, Mehmed was obliged to retreat.

Mihaloğlu Ali Bey's raiders, who advanced from the back right wing of the Ottoman army to the front, and Iskender Bey's raiders, who advanced from the back left to the front, were ruining the Ak Koyunlu army and chasing them. The Ottoman army's striking force, the Janissaries, hadn't even touched their swords while the Ak Koyunlu army was already dispersed from all sides.

Uzun Hasan realized that there was no chance left for him, and once he learned that his son Zeynel was dead, he started to run away in order to save his own life. He was telling Karamanoğlu Pir Ahmed Bey, "Karaman-oğlu! May your dynasty be ruined. You led me to lose my dear and so many soldiers. What I had to do with the Ottomans?" Uzun Hasan covered a distance of three days in one day, and after he reached the headquarters, he took his family with him and took the road of Tabriz.

Although the majority of the Ottoman statesman proposed to go to Tabriz and destroy the Ak Koyunlu state so they would not dare again to attack the Ottoman land, but Fatih Sultan Mehmed rejected this proposal by saying:

"Persecuting the malefactor called Uzun Hasan was the aim of the sultanate. This was fulfilled. Destroying his dynasty is not bravery. Cutting of the head of his intractable son is enough to spark the fever in his heart. It is necessary to shed the blood of his family with our shiny sword. What was done to him is enough. Destroying the dynasty of the Muslim sultans is not a good tradition. If it was up to me I wouldn't even do that much for my sultanate. But he was the reason for that. Our aim was to discipline him. That was largely fulfilled. Going after him with the inducement of revenge will lead to destroy and pulverize many places. And we would be the subject of the malediction of the poor, the rich, and plenty of oppressed people. You know that even the sky can't be a shield for the oppressed ones calls. Being target to that is not an act of who thinks about his end. Being responsible for such a great burden, and busy with infertile acts by suspending the holy war with the Christians is not the aim of those who carry concern for the hereafter."

Those indications of Fatih clearly reveal the real aims of the Ottoman state about conquest and war.

The message of peace brought by the messenger of Ak Koyunlu to Şebinkarahisar was accepted in the condition of not attacking the Ottoman land. The year after, Uzun Hasan informed with the same messenger who he sent to Istanbul that he would never abuse the Ottoman land again. This victory saved the country, which was enclosed from the east to the west, and was in a critical situation from a great crisis. It prevented a defeat that might cause it to split up. The Crusader spirit that was inflamed by the Pope and the plan of their allies in the east was failed. Thus, a complete domination was established on the land situated in the west of Euphrates River after the Otlukbeli Victory. At the same time, the Crusaders and especially the Venetians, lost almost their complete hope about winning the long war that they declared against the Ottomans.

In 1474 another expedition was made against the Karamanlides, who cooperated with the Venetians in the Otlukbeli War, and attacked Ottoman land. Shahzada Mustafa, who was suffering from kidney disease for a long time, fell sick during this expedition and lost his life. This incident deeply saddened the sultan. After the expedition, Gedik Ahmed Pasha took Central Anatolia under control and all the attention was turned back to the western front.

STEP BY STEP TO THE DOMINATION
OF THE MEDITERRANEAN SEA

I n the summer of 1469 the Venetian navy, who took advantage from the Ottoman expedition to the Karama-nid land, arrived at the Rumeli coast and looted the rich commercial city Enez. They took back the islands Lemnos and Imbros and also conquered some castles in Mora.

The sultan didn't delay responding the attack. In January 1469, in the middle of the winter, he sent raiders to Europe. This great raid was achieved by ten thousand soldiers, who were led by the Bosnian flag officer, Isa Bey. Not only Venice, but also Germany and Austria were ruined. According to Italian and Austrian documents, Nicolae Yorga reported, "those were the world's most defi-ant soldiers, they came as if they were flying in the sky."

In the following year, the sultan took action, and he directed his attention to Euboea Island, which has an extremely important strategic place. The island was on the route of the Turkish crafts that were shipping out between Mora and Anatolia. The pirates that attacked the Anato-lian coasts and the Ottoman crafts and the Venetian crafts were taking refuge there.

Euboea was first blockaded by one hundred galleys, two hundred little naval boats and transport vessels led by Mahmut Pasha. And Fatih surrounded the castle after passing through a huge bridge that was settled in the Euboea Bosporus through Thessaly. Although the Venetian navy came to support Euboea, they couldn't approach the island because of the blockade. Finally, on July 11, 1470, after a violent attack, the Euboea Castle was taken.

In 1471, Gedik Ahmed Pasha was sent to the Karamanlides. The sultan, who was aware of the alliance between the Ak Koyunlu and the Venetians, proposed peace to the Venetians in order to disturb this plan and avoid a new crusade. Also a defensive status was taken against the Hungarians. Rumeli raiders were not sent to Hungary, but rather to its rival, the Austrian Empire and a peace proposal was made. The Hungarian messenger that would come was going to be delayed until the end of the Otlukbeli War.

Meanwhile, in the summer of 1472, the crusader navy, led by the Venetians, landed at the Mediterranean coast and settled down in the coast of Izmir and Antalya in order to support the Karamanlides and Uzun Hasan.

The Ottomans' victory from the Otlukbeli War in the summer of 1473 changed the balance in favor of the Ottomans. Hopelessness and deep cracks occurred in the Crusade coalition about winning this long and hard competition that was ongoing for more than ten years. The Hungarian messenger's requests were rejected after he was delayed until the end of the Eastern Expedition due to the Otlukbeli victory. Hungary couldn't take advantage of this chance as it was at war with the King of Poland in 1473 while the Ottomans were in the Eastern expedition.

The light forces of cavalry, who were organized in the borderland of Rumeli, were attacking the enemy with sudden raids in order to batter "Akıncılar" (raiders). Those units didn't only organize sudden raids, but they also took on a task of intelligence, collecting information about the situation, the methods, and the power of the enemy.

The raiders provided intelligence service during the war; they scanned the enemy's land and open ways, and dismiss the possible ambushes. Besides that they also protected the crops that were on the army's path, collected information about the enemies, and ensured the security of places like bridges and passages. They would proceed in advance of the main army about four or five days' distance. The horses that they would ride were fast and resistant, all chosen according to their task. When they went for an expedition they used to take two or three horses to remount with them, and leave the horses that are tired with their hosts. On their way back they loaded those horses with pillaged goods and captives. Ten raiders were led by a corporal, one hundred raiders were led by a lieutenant, and one thousand raiders were led by a major. On the top of the hierarchical chain was "Akıncı Beyi" (raider chief). Some of the raider chiefs who had the high rank of *sancak-*

beyi (flag chief) had extraordinary authorizations and they took orders directly from the sultan.

The raiders were not centrally led, but were organized on borderlines. Each region had its own commandant and the raiders were named after the family name of their commandant. Malkoçoğlu raiders were organized in Silistra, Turhanlı raiders were organized in Mora, and Mihaloğlu raiders were organized in the region of Smederevo.

The names, appearance, and manner of the raiders were registered in records; a copy of these records was kept in the registry of the capital and the other one was kept in the province where they were or in the *sanjak kadiluk* (a local administrative subdivision) to avoid any kind of corruption. After each expedition, agile, good cavaliers and strong youngsters joined the Akıncı Corps to replace the martyrs and disabled ones. According to Akıncı law, those whose fathers were raiders got priority to be chosen, and those who did not have a guarantor weren't registered.

The number of raiders who were in the Ottoman state wasn't precisely known. It is estimated that until the fifteenth century, their number was about forty thousand. Due to an inspection made in 1559, the Turhanlı raiders numbered about seven thousand. The Akıncıs were using swords, shields, machetes, spears, and maces, as long as these items did not prevent them from moving fast, and generally they weren't wearing armor. The most senior members of the corps were the ones who mostly crossed the Danube. One of the most famous raiders of Fatih's epoch, Mihaloğlu Ali Bey, crossed the Danube more than three hundred and thirty times during his life.

We can summarize the raiding techniques of those intrepid cavaliers as: the Akıncı army used to break into several branches in the intended area. In the actions moving forward, the army would split into smaller groups. Each group's target was previously determined. Those groups reunited upon their return. The reuniting point was a different place than the area where the army split up. With the unification of all the branches, a whole army was formed. This situation had a terrifying and horrible effect on the enemies; hundreds of myths were told about where the Akıncıs were situated and where they attacked.

The greatest principle of the Akıncıs was not to face the enemy's army and avoid the battlefield as long as it was not necessary. The battlefields were fought by the regular army, not by the raiders. The exception to this what when it was important to gain intelligence. According to Babinger's indication, the Turks were immediately informed about what was planned in the meetings that were organized in Germany and Hungary and they used to change their plans according to this information. For example, the German authorities took precaution in the whole Bavarian region and informed clearly that there was a Turkish spy who was leaking information, but this "man who has a rough coat and rides a small horse from city to city as Saint Valentine" was never arrested. Most of the spies were members of the Akıncıs and they spoke foreign languages very well. Among the intelligence service there were native people too.

"WE WERE AS JOYFUL AS CHILDREN IN EXPEDITIONS OF A THOUSAND CAVALIERS"

Sultan Mehmed responded to the alliance of Venice Republic with the Karamanlides and the Ak Koyunlu, which was aiming to compress the Ottomans from Asia, by allying with the rival of Venice, the Republic of Florence. Also the raiders were working underground in Venice in an attempt to damage its economic life. After eliminating the Eastern wing of the alliance with the victory that was obtained from Otlukbeli Pitched Battle in 1473, the Albanian castles Korya and Les were taken. Venice's most important base, the Republic of Shkoder, was encircled by Fatih himself. Deterrent expeditions were organized on Venetian land, Hungary, Austria, and Poland, which were on the other side of the Danube through Albania. These intimidating actions that were led by Ottoman raiders were depolarizing the economic and psychological state of Venice and its allies. "For years not even a cock crowed in the places where the Akıncıs had passed."

Continuing with this strategy, in the winter of 1474, Mihaloğlu Ali Bey rapidly took action, with eighteen thousand *serdengeçtis* (bouncers) under his command. Varadin was seized and looted in this great Hungarian expedition. This expedition was the greatest operation realized in the Carniolan province. This expedition was started after the Croatian feudal lords asked for help from the House of Frankopan, and the raiders entered Carniol through Croatia. They also appeared at Ljubljana, which was the center of Slovenia. Another branch proceeded to Klagenfurt. The enemy's cavaliers were defeated and two thousand persons were captured, which also included the nobles of the city. The other group, which went from Carinthia to Styria, was seen at Gor. If we consider that ninety thousand animals and sixty thousand people captivated, we will be able to understand the enemy's great economic and military loss.

In 1474 another raider unit entered Polish land and ruined Podolia and Galicia. In the same year the flag officer of Smederevo, Malkoçoğlu Balı Bey, led an operation to Ardeal. "Balı Bey who had fire of enthusiasm in his eyes" passed Danube and spread fear in Petrovaradin.

A new expedition was organized to Istinia and Caranthia. Ahmed Pasha defeated the enemy in the Battle of Rann and proceeded to Carniolan.

In 1477, the governor of Bosnia, Iskender Pasha, organized a great expedition to Northern Italy. The rich Venetian plain was ruined after the expedition passed through Isonzo and Tagliamento. The Akıncıs watered their horses at Piave and turned back from Friuli.

Fifteen thousand people joined the Venice expedition through Friuli in 1478. Mihaloğlu Ali and Malkoçoğlu Balı Beys were also ready in the army that was led by Iskender Pasha. After Friuli, Gorizia was also seized and the number of the raiders reached thirty thousand when they reached Isonzo. Fifteen thousand raiders passed to Isonzo, which is called Aksu by the Turks, and the others were fighting from the other side of the river. The region was so steep that people could not pass on foot, and the raiders were jumping with their horses over cliffs and rocks. Those scary operations that brought fear to the Venetian plain, brought Venice, which was running out resources, to its knees. In a letter written by Celso Maffei to Andrea Vendramin, we understand that Venice was exhausted after this war: "The enemy is in our doors. The axe touched the roots of the tree. If God's help doesn't reach us, the axe will cut the roots." According to Babinger, the Venetians, who tried every way to stop the Ottomans, organized fourteen assassination attempts on Fatih from 1454 to 1479, but none were successful.

With the death of Uzun Hasan in the same year, Venice had depleted all the hopes. The economic crises and hunger reached its highest level. In 1478's expedition, the Ottoman raiders arrived exactly before the harvest and they left the Venetians hungry that winter. The Venetians, who were used to live in prosperity and security, were fed up with the Turkish cavaliers who were moving like thunderbolts around throughout summer and winter. People left their homes and lived in trenches and shelters that they dug out of the soil. The public, who was fed up with the wars that were continuing for sixteen years, was pressing the government for peace at any price. Those expeditions were sucking all the economic resources of the country. Those expeditions brought Hungary and Venice to their knees and delivered the final blow. The Republic of Venice sent Giovanni Dario, who was the most talented diplomat of that epoch and knew the Turks very well, with unusual "unlimited authorities" never seen in its history to Istanbul for a peace proposal.

The Great War that was continuing since 1463 was finally over with the agreement signed on January 25, 1479, at Venice's request. The Ottoman state succeeded to defeat all the armies of the big coalition in the seas, in the east and the west, by using all the economic, political, and military possibilities. The most powerful state of the coalition, the Republic of Venice, was strictly liquidated with the Ak Koyunlu. Delaying some of the enemies with attractive peace proposals with various excuses in times of hardship and war, than once this tactic resulted in victory on the other fronts. Fatih used this strategy to finish the delayed state, which shows us that he wasn't only a good marshal, but also a talented diplomat.

According to the agreement, Venice was going to evacuate Albania, Mora, and the islands, and the sultan was going to give back the Dalmatian coast. Venice accepted to pay a yearly tax of ten thousand gold coins, its old debt, which was one hundred thousand ducat, and two hundred thousand ducat as war compensation. The Venetian traders were going to be able to trade freely in the Ottoman land. So Fatih Sultan Mehmed was aiming to revive the Ottoman economy and tear Venice from the Crusaders. Thus Venice was sent away from Albania, Mora, and the North Aegean; the only dominant power left south of the Danube was the Ottoman state. The Balkan nations preferred Ottoman governance to Catholic governance. According to the statements of Ottoman chroniclers, this victory, which was obtained by "supporting the pigs against the dogs and the dogs against the pigs," was opening the doors of a bright future.

The Istanbul Peace Treaty was affirmed by the Venetian doge on San Marco day, April 25, 1479, and declared to the public. The Ottoman messenger who was sent to get a copy of the agreement affirmed by the doge Lütfi Bey signed another secret agreement with Venice. According to that secret agreement, if one of the two states went to war with any European state, Venice would supply one hundred naval ships and the Ottomans will supply one hundred thousand cavaliers. The Ottoman sultan, who was planning to conquer Italy, was pacified and put Venice in an extremely complicated situation regarding the European policy.

The Ottomans, who were free from the Venetian side, started to pay more attention to Central Europe. The time came to defeat Germany, Austria, Hungary, and

Poland. On August 24, 1479, the Turkish raiders passed the Bosnian border and scanned the southern area of the Danube plain between Budapest and Bratislava. This operation, realized with a full squad formed of three thousand raiders, is one of the greatest expeditions in Ottoman history.

A Janissary soldier

For this expedition that was aiming to damage the gold and silver mines in Transylvania, twelve flag officers were leading the units that branched out as they proceeded north. The most famous Akıncı governors like Mihaloğlu İskender Bey, Malkoçoğlu Balıbey, Evrenosoğlu İsa Bey, and Evrenosoğlu Hasan Bey served along Mihaloğlu Ghazi Alaadin Ali Pasha, who undertook the command of this operation. They didn't hesitate to fight pitched battles from time to time because of the crowded army. This expedition tyrannized Germany, Austria, and Hungary, and caused serious casualties for the Turks too; nearly twenty thousand raiders were left in the green valleys of Hungary. The biggest pitched battle of this expedition took place in Kenyermezo valley called "Kelle Vadisi" (Head Valley) situated between the Carpathians and Marose Riverin on October 13, 1479.

The raiders, who wanted to take their revenge from their losses in the expedition of 1479, took action again in 1480. On July 29, a group of raiders attacked the Carniolan province while another group of the army ran over Styria. They entered towns that were on the way. Another branch of the Akıncıs reached Graz. Even the people of Munich weren't feeling safe anymore. A militia unit was formed by 1600 people and a little cannon was placed on the tower of Saint Peter's Church, after the decision of the city council.

THE SULTAN WHO TRANSFORMED
THE SEA TO A LAKE

After Istanbul was conquered, Galata, which was a Genoese colony, joined the Ottoman state, and the Genoese were allowed to trade freely in the Ottoman land. In the following years the Black Sea and the surrounding areas were going to be dominated and the Black Sea was going to be closed to all other states and almost transformed to a "Turkish lake" according to a certain plan. So the Ottomans were going to become the only ruler of the commerce of this region, an extremely animated region, and condemn the European states to their own economies.

The trade routes that started from Astrakhan, Kabul, and Urgench were passing through the Black Sea in order to reach Europe. The silk that came from the Caspian Sea, and the spices from India were distributed from this port. The ships were also transporting trade commodities such as wheat, fur, leather, wax, fish, salt, and caviar from this region. The Ottoman historian Kemal Pashazada described Feodosia and the commercial viability as: "A magnificent city built in the cost of the northern region of the Black Sea. Traders were visiting from overseas and over deserts. The Tatars of the Crimean land, the Circassians, and the unbeliever Russians used to gather there and trade."

In 1454, Feodosia, which was the center of the Genoese colonies in the Black Sea, was oppressed with the Khan of Crimea so the Genoese Republic was obliged to pay taxes to the Ottomans and the Crimean Khanate. In the same year the Ottoman navy threatened Akkerman and demanded extortion from the governor of Bogdan. Due to the great importance of Akkerman for the future of the northern European commerce and its localization linked to the Black Sea and the straits, the king of Bogdan accepted to pay taxes and the dependence to the Ottomans in return for free trade in the Ottoman land. In 1456 the Empire of Trebizond also accepted to pay taxes, so all the states of the Black Sea coast submitted the Ottoman domination.

In the next phase, Fatih was willing to establish the direct domination of the Ottomans on all those states. Accordingly Amasra, Sinop, and Trabzon, that is to say the Black Sea, was going to be under the domination of the Anatolian coasts. But as of 1463, the Ottomans who had to struggle with the Crusade coalition led by Venice and the Karamanlides and the Ak Koyunlu from the east, couldn't concern themselves with the northern costs of the Black Sea for several years.

The most serious rival for the domination of the Black Sea seemed to be the Genoese, who were well-established in the Crimean region by dint of their commerce with Lithuania, the rulers of Polish Yagellons. The Genoese, the voivode of Bogdan, the Khan of Crimea, and the Yagellons, who were aware of the Ottomans' objectives about the Black Sea, were in cooperation with each other against the Turks.

The sultan sent the navy to Feodosia in 1469, and raised Feodosia's taxes in 1470. After the Yagellons allied with the Golden Horde against the Khan of Crimea, the Crimeans felt the need to approach to the Grand Duchy of Moscow and the Ottoman Empire. The voivode of Bogdan Stephan Cel Mare declared dependence to the Yagellons and stopped paying taxes to the Ottomans. The voivode defeated the Crimean forces, which entered Bogdan at 1469. He also took advantage of the attack of the Ottoman army, with the attendance of Mihaloğlu raiders, on Uzun Hasan in 1473 and dismissed Radul, who was dependent on the Ottomans from the Wallachian throne, and replaced him with his man. He refused to deliver the Genoese captives to the Ottomans. He defeated the seigneur of Rumelia, Suleiman Pasha's army that was sent to him in the winter January 17, 1475. The prince of Bogdan was called "Jesus's Fighter." Fatih decided to advance on Cel Mare by himself. But his aggravated disease prevented him from doing that.

Meanwhile the chaos was increasing in Crimea and the khanate forces approached Istanbul, so Gedik Ahmed Pasha was sent immediately to an expedition with the navy, and in June 1475 Feodosia was taken back. The Feodosians left the *takfur* hopeless by saying:

"We don't have the possibility to protect and save this fort from the Turks. If they take it from us by force they would kill us all. They would capture our children and loot our assets. Rather than that, let's give it to them nicely. Because those Turks built every place that they took it nicely. They didn't ruin it. The Ottoman tradition is forgiving who come to their heel and is not hurting their children, and behaving in a friendly manner."

All the Genoese colonies were seized. Later, the Castle of Azov and Menguğ were also seized. Meñli I Giray, who was captured by the Genoese in Sudak, signed a document that declared his dependence on the Ottomans and was declared as "Crimea Khan" again.

The Crimean army, which was formed by good and fearless cavaliers who were resistant to every kind of trouble faced during expeditions, was going to oppress Russia, Poland, and Europe. The Ottoman sultans used to emphasize in their threatening edicts that they are coming with Tatar soldiers, which are as crowded as the stars in the sky. From the other side the chaos ended; peace, security, and stability took over Crimea, which was taken under the Ottomans' protection. The Crimean state was politically, economically, and culturally developed. The

Khanate of Astragan and Kasim fell prey to Russia in a short time because of their inner fights, and the Crimeans were going to live in peace and security for three hundred years until 1783.

Fatih, who strengthened his power in the north of the Black Sea after seizing the Crimean Khanate, started bombarding the coasts of Bogdan with the navy that he routed through the Black Sea. In 1476 he entered Bogdan with the Crimean and the Wallachian armies. Stephan Cel Mare had chosen a big forest called "Ocean of Trees" as a line of defense. He surrounded the area with shields and ditches and placed obstacles from trees and carriages in the back. And he placed cannons in the front so the forest was almost transformed into a fort. Polish and Hungarian chosen units joined his army, which was formed by twenty thousand soldiers. The war started on July 26 with mutual cannon shots. The courageous soldiers of Anatolia and Rumelia started to attack the enemy with swords like fire. But they couldn't pass the shields and ditches. The Janissaries, who were driven back, couldn't proceed because of the cannon shots and failed to act. The sultan was worried about this situation of those courageous fighters who used to face the cannons and guns without fear, and said, "Those boys did something very strange. Do the courageous fighters act like that?" then rode his horse on the enemy. The Ottoman army was livened up and gathered all its strength, and stood for the cannon and gun shots, and flowed as a flood on the enemy.

The soldiers of the voivode were killed by the swords of the *ghazis* in this war that lasted for ten hours. Stephan Cel Mare was defeated in Alba Valea and couldn't be captured because he ran away.

While Fatih was planning to seize all the forts of Bogdan in the Black Sea, he came to know that the Hungarians were preparing to attack Smederevo. And he returned back, saying, "Protecting a Muslim land is better than seizing a heathen fort." The request of the voivode of Bogdan about raising his taxes from three thousand gold to six thousand gold and his promises about being the friend of the Ottomans' friends and the enemy of their enemies was accepted and he was taken again under the Ottomans' domination. After the navy that was sent in 1479 seized Taman and Circassia the domination of the Black Sea was substantially completed.

A Definite Solution
for Rhodes

I n 1291, the Knights of Saint John, who were sent off from Acre Castle by the Mamluks, settled to Rhodes Island that was in the hands of the Byzantine Empire. Later they also seized the islands Dodecanese, Ikaria, and Kasota, and the ports of Bodrum and Izmir. The Mamluk state, which was the ruler of the eastern region of the Mediterranean in the fifteenth century, realized the importance of Cyprus and Rhodes for the security of the East Mediterranean coasts and oppressed these two islands constantly. After three expeditions realized in 1424, 1425, and 1426, the king of Cyprus accepted to pay taxes to the Mamluks. The Mamluks couldn't seize Rhodes after expeditions realized in 1440, 1443, and 1445. During those expeditions, Fatih's father, Murad II, was on the Ottoman throne.

In Fatih Sultan Mehmed's period, two expeditions were realized in 1455 and 1467, but the island resisted and couldn't be seized. The pope supported the cavaliers of Rhodes materially and spiritually, donations made to the sect reached astronomical numbers, and cavaliers selected from every nation rushed to defend the island.

Fatih's tughra

Sultan Mehmed, who was preparing to seize Italy, didn't want to leave an unsolved knot behind and he sent a navy led by Mesih Pasha from Gallipoli with the order of definitive conquest. The navy anchored in front of Rhodes in May 23, 1480. Another navy, led by Gedik Ahmed Pasha, started to drop soldiers to the Italian coasts on July 28 when the general attack was initiated. The enemy was deeply damaged by explosive demolition bombs, which were used for the first time, and the Ottoman soldiers who were attacking as "unchained lions." Although the flag of Mesih Pasha was planted at the tower of the castle, the seized lands couldn't be kept because of the dissension that occurred between Mesih Pasha and his soldiers. The army, which lost nine thousand martyrs and five thousand wounded, receded after the soldiers turned against fighting. The navies that embarked with the soldiers left Rhodes on August 3. After this failure the sultan didn't even allow Mesih Pasha to enter Istanbul. As soon as he approached

Beşiktaş, he was dismissed as vizier and sent to Gallipoli as a flag officer.

The main reasons for the failure of the siege was that the island wasn't completely surrounded, and the arrival of support from Europe. Thus with the lessons taken from Sultan Suleiman siege and the necessary actions, Rhodes was going to be seized in 1521.

THE BALANCE OF POWER IS CHANGING
IN THE MEDITERRANEAN REGION

A new agreement was signed between the Ottomans and the Republic of Dubrovnik-Ragusa, which was one of the states that had a strategic importance in the Adriatic Sea. The Republic of Dubrovnik accepted the raising of its taxes without any rejection and was connected to Istanbul with stronger ties.

The islands Zante, Kefalonia, and Ayamavr, which are known as Ionian Islands, were legally dependent to the Republic of Venice through the dynasty of Tocco and were paying taxes to the Ottomans at the same time. This status of the islands was allowing them to be annexed without fighting Venice. Venice was somehow accepting that those islands were relating to the Turks by acknowledging the fact that they paid taxes to the Ottomans. Also in the 1479 Agreement of Istanbul, Ionia was excluded from the scope of the islands, which meant that Venice partly approved that those lands didn't belong to it.

. At the same time, the marriage of the last ducat Leonardo with the princess of Napoli made the Venetian doge suspicious. If the ruler of Strait of Taranto Napoli would seize the Ionian Islands, the actions of Venice in the Adriatic might be restricted.

After that, Gedik Ahmed Pala was assigned to the conquest of the Ionian Islands. The islands Zante, Kefalonia, and Ayamavr were seized without the need for war. In 1480, Leonardo took his treasure and fled to Napoli. Venice wasn't in a position to appeal this situation. Sixteen years of war had just ended. They were in state of war with Napoli and they weren't on good terms with the other Italian states. Plus they probably wouldn't like to see the Akıncıs again in the Venetian valleys.

THE SOUND OF THE AKINCIS IN
THE APENNINE PENINSULA

The spies, who had been supplying information from Italy for a long time, were indicating that the situation was pretty convenient to take action. The conditions were suitable for attacking Italy that was having problems because of the political rivalry between the Papal State, Venice, Napoli, and the reactions against the political attempts of the Papal State. The Ottoman commanders of Bosnia and Mora were also briefing that it was the right moment to take action. The flag officer of Bosnia, Mihaloğlu Iskender Bey, was indicating in the letter that he sent to the capital how this region was rich and valuable although those who protected it were weak by the following words; "This land of Apuglia has a lot of honey but few bees. All the states around desire it. May Allah the Almighty succeed the puissant sultan. Amin, O Lord of the worlds!" Fatih Sultan Mehmed, who built an integrated empire, ruled from one center situated between the Euphrates and the Danube by defeating his greatest rivals in Balkan and the east and realized his plan, which had been designed for thirty years, and took action to realize his dream project.

The Ottoman navy formed of one hundred forty pieces left Gallipoli, and left Vlorë which was the last supply base on July 26, 1480, towards Italy. Eighteen thousand infantry landed at Otranto after covering seventy-five kilometers of distance. So the Turks started the invasion of Italy by the heel of the boot. An Akıncı unit formed by one thousand people was sent into the inner parts of Italy for an exploration. The enemy was caught unaware and unprepared. Meanwhile the army of the Pope and his ally the King of Napoli were at war with Florence. Florence was supported by a Turkish messenger. Although the son of Ferdinand the king of Napoli, Prince Alfonso, resisted the landing of Gedik Ahmed Pasha, he was obliged to flee after his army was defeated. The Apennine Peninsula was shocked on August 11, 1480, after the news that the fortified Otranto Castle was seized.

Ahmed Pasha sent one of the groups of his army that was divided to Brindisi and the other group to Taranto. The king of Napoli left Florence and rushed back to defend Apuglia. On September 8 the army of Napoli arrived at Apuglia. The army led by Ferdinand waited for days before fighting with the Turks. Ahmed Pasha transmitted that if Apuglia would not be surrendered by peace the sultan would come with one hundred peons, eighteen thousand cavaliers, and unprecedented sized cannons in order to ruin the State of Napoli. Ferdinand informed the Pope and the other kings that if a great help didn't come he has no chance but to resign.

The Pope, who described how the situation was critical, invited all the kings to unite against this danger, and the war with Florence was terminated. With the papal edict all the European churches and on All Saints Day prayers were performed in order to defeat the Turks. The king of England, Edward IV, informed the Vatican that he would not join the Crusades by writing in his letter that: "he doesn't see the possibility of the Ottomans passing the English Channel and that he has nothing to do with the Turks." The dissemination of Mesih Pasha's Rhodes Expedition increased fear and worry in Europe. Pope Sixtus IV, who was feeling at a stalemate, was considering carrying his post to France. Medallions were prepared in Florence and Ferrera for Fatih. In the medallion of Ferrera, it said, "Sultan Mehmed Descendant of Osman the emperor of the Turks and East Rome" was written.

The Republic of Venice recognized the rights of Fatih Sultan Mehmed in southern Italy officially through its ambassador Gritti in Istanbul. The south of Italy previously belonged to the Byzantines and now Fatih Sultan Mehmed was on the throne of the Eastern Roman Empire.

The plans of the king of Florence was as follows: Central and Southern Italy was going to be dependent on Fatih, and Northern Italy was going to be liable to Fatih. The Spanish dynasty was going to be dismissed, and the Pope was going to stay in Rome having the status of the Patriarchate of Istanbul. And the land of the papacy that was in Central Italy was going to be left to Florence.

This new status of The Apennine Peninsula might have led to very dangerous and grave results for the Republic of Venice, because the seventy-five-kilometer long strait between Vlorë and Otranto was going to be under Ottoman domination. The transitions made through the straits, which meant the entrances and exits of the Mediterranean, were going to be liable to Ottoman authority. That meant the death of the Mediterranean commerce of Venice, which had a vital importance. If it couldn't practice commerce in the Mediterranean, it would be no different from the central states. This new conjuncture might ruin the Republic of Venice. One last formula for salvation was left for the Republic of Venice, which was in an extremely desperate situation: Achieving the assassination that was tried and failed fourteen times (according to Babinger)!

TENSION IN THE RELATIONS BETWEEN
THE OTTOMANS AND THE MAMLUKS

The Mamluk state (1250–1517) was founded in 1249 by Kipchak commander Aybak who took over the throne after killing the last ruler of the Ayyubids Turan Shah in a bloody riot. With time, the state dominated the Egyptian and Syrian lands and became the most powerful state of the region. After the Mongols dismissed the Abbasid state in 1258, which was situated in Baghdad, by invading the Islamic world and killing the last Abbasid Caliph, the last Caliph's uncle Al-Mustansir, who survived the massacre, fled with his family to Cairo. The fact that the institution of the caliphate was taken under the protection of the Mamluk state raised respect for the Mamluks in the Islamic world.

After the Mamluks stopped the Mongol invasion to the west in the Battle of Jalut in Palestine, they caused great joy in the Islamic world. This victory that was gained against the Mongols, who made all the Muslims suffer from Central Asia to the Middle East, raised the prestige of the Mamluk State. Cleaning the rest of the Crusades in the Middle East elevated the Mamluks to the protectors and leaders of the Islamic world. The Mamluks established peace, serenity, and stability in the Middle East for ages between the fourteenth and fifteenth centuries, which led the Eastern Mediterranean ports to progress and become the central region of the spice trade. This situation led the Mamluks, who were rising from the religious and political aspects, to strengthen economically too.

The relationship between the Mamluks and the Ottomans, who entered the stage of history in the fourteenth century in the west of Anatolia, started extremely well. The Ottomans' efforts and holy wars to spread Islam in the Balkans and be the active representative of Islam in the west was appreciated by the Mamluks just as it was appreciated by the Islamic world. After the victories achieved against the Crusades in Rumelia by Murad I and Yıldırım Bayezid and especially the victory of Nicopolis, the caliph of Egypt Mamluks sent gifts to Yıldırım and gave him the title of "Sultan-ı İklim-i Rum" (The Sultan of the Byzantine Region). But the policy of spreading towards the Euphrates led by Yıldırım, the seizing of Malatya, which belonged to the Mamluks, the conquest of Elbistan, and the choice of Dulkadiroğulları, who was the liege of the Mamluks, to be dependent to the Ottomans, overturned relations between the two states. Because of that tension, the Mamluks joined Timur in the difficult War of Ankara against Yıldırım Bayezid although they were disturbed by the Timur's policies. However, in the epoch of Çelebi Mehmed and Murad II, the relationship of the Ottomans and Mamluks was normalized again.

In the period of Fatih Sultan Mehmed the Ottoman-Mamluk relations were undulating; unstable but always tense. In the early years of his sultanate, relations progressed in a positive direction; the conquest edicts that were sent from Istanbul to Cairo after conquering Istanbul and the other Balkan expeditions were replied to by the Mamluk caliphs with congratulatory edicts. Even though the successful holy war and jihad activities of the Ottomans were causing unpleasantness in the Palace of Cairo, this news brought extreme joy to the people. After the Conquest of Istanbul, festivals that lasted for days were organized in Cairo. But after 1460 the two states started to fall out deeply. For example, although Fatih Sultan Mehmed attained a victory from the Expedition of Trabzon, the Mamluks didn't congratulate this victory, and responding to that, the sultan didn't congratulate Khuchqadam when he became a monarch.

One of the issues that disrupted the relations between the Ottoman and Mamluk was the Hejaz waterways matter. After that the Ottoman pilgrims who went to the holy lands in order to perform the Pilgrimage complained about how the water wells were neglected and dilapidated and how they suffered from that, the sultan set his hands to that. But the officials who were sent by the Ottoman State to fix the water wells and waterways were not well received by the Egyptians and were humiliated and sent back. Meanwhile the Karamanlides took advantage of this situation and sent a messenger to the sultan of Egypt informing him that the sultan encouraged the Emir of Mecca to rebel by subsidizing him. Those events were considered by the Mamluk state as interference in its internal affairs.

Another factor that raised the tension between the two countries was the contestation of dominating the principality of Dulkadiroğulları. Fatih was aware of the strategic importance of the principality for the spread of the Ottoman State to the south. But the Mamluks wanted to protect the buffer zone with the Ottoman state, which was becoming stronger and more enlarged. The principality of Dulkadiroğulları became a region of power struggle of the Ak Koyunlar, the Mamluks, and the Ottomans. After the Mamluks posted Shah Budak as a seignior for the principality of Dulkadiroğulları, responding to that, the Ottomans supported Shahsuvar Bey. With that support Shahsuvar Bey took over the control of the principality. The Ottoman-Mamluk relations seemed to get seriously intense in this phase. Shahsuvar Bey wasn't contented with that, but he also seized Darende, which belonged to the Mamluks. And he started to influence the emirs of Aleppo and Damascus. Fatih was secretly supporting those activities in order to enlarge his impact area in Syria. Meanwhile the bad treatment that both the Mamluks and the Ottomans showed to the messengers sent raised the tension to higher levels. But the Ottomans cut off support to Shahsuvar Bey because he broke his promises. Shahsuvar Bey, who lost the support of Fatih, was defeated against the Mamluk army in Antep and was hung after being captured. Killing Shahsuvar Bey, breaking the promises made to the Ottomans, and beheading some of the Ottoman soldiers, and having people play with their heads in the public square of Cairo revealed the hostility of the Mamluks. But in the meantime Fatih delayed the issue of Egypt as he was in state of war with the Venetians in the west and with Uzun Hasan and the Karamanlides in the east. After dismissing the alliance between the Ak Koyunlu and the Karamanlides and finishing the war with the coalition states led by the Republic of Venice, in 1480 Fatih focused all his attention on the Mamluks.

We know precisely the aims of Fatih's policies in Europe, the Aegean, and Black Sea, but we can only guess the ultimate objective of his southern policies. We understand that he wanted to establish an economically powerful empire that ruled a wide area through his policy. In the years when the Cape of Good Hope was not yet discovered and the trade paths hadn't moved to the oceans, and when we consider that Egyptian and Syrian ports were situated in the center of the spice routes, it is pretty normal that Fatih wanted to rule the region. Bringing about the attempt to seize the Dulkadiroğulları and Hijaz waterways matter can be considered as excuses for this larger objective. Seizing the land of Dulkadir before walking on Egypt and using it as a stepping-stone in the period of Yavuz Selim may ease estimating Fatih's plans. It is also conceivable that he wanted to eliminate the Mamluk State in order to establish a strong influence on the Islamic world and race to the top. It is a fact that he had the ideal of uniting the west and east under a single roof. It also possible that the Mamluks, who were aware of the developments and the envisagement of Fatih, were trying to sustain the existence of the principality of Dulkadiroğulları, which was considered a buffer zone for possible operations that may have accrued in the future. On the other hand the fact that the Mamluks increased war preparations by guessing that this tension that was rising was going to result with war, might make it easier to predict the future objectives of the sultan. But the death of Fatih Sultan Mehmed on May 3, 1481, during an expedition prevented a possible Ottoman-Mamluk war.

"LA GRANDE AQUILA A MORTA!"

Fatih Sultan Mehmed, who took action from Üsküdar in the spring of 1481, demanded that the Anatolian soldiers gather in the Konya Basin, and sent Shahzada Cem, the governor of Karaman, to the Syrian border. The target of this expedition wasn't known. But it was obvious that the target was a far country considering the comprehensive preparations. The general opinion of Ottoman historians was that this expedition was targeting the Mamluks. In fact, the historian of Fatih's period states that, "The direction of the expedition was known as the Anatolian side, but was it to the Arabs or the Persians that wasn't known." Also Mehmed Nashri Effendi indicates that, "No one knew the target of the expedition, which started from Gebze." But as he used to do sometimes, maybe he aimed to prevent the preparation of the enemy by sending the forces to the east. Which means maybe he wanted to seize Rhodes or complete the conquest of Italy that he already started, because there was no obstacle to prevent him from conquering Rome and the Vatican. But in the event that he lost, the Crusades might dismiss the Ottomans from Otranto, and the strategic bridgehead Puglia, which had been seized, might be lost and the operation might fail.

The Fatih Mosque that was constructed by Fatih Sultan Mehmed

Wherever this expedition was targeting, it remained inconclusive by the death of Fatih in Hünkar Çayırı near Gebze (May 3, 1481). The corpse of the sultan, which was brought to Istanbul, was inhumed in his mausoleum in Fatih Mosque after performing the funeral prayer.

The death of the sultan, who was only forty-nine, caused much sadness in Muslim and Ottoman lands; the ambassador of Venice in Istanbul wrote in a letter he sent to Italy, "La Grande Aquila a Morta" (The Great Eagle died). This good news enraptured Italy, which was suffering from hopelessness, and cannons were fired and festivals were organized in the whole of Italy. Especially

Rome and the Vatican witnessed extreme demonstrations of joy. The Pope ordered to ring the bells three days and nights, and to "make thanksgiving rituals" in the whole of Europe.

The famous German historian Franz Babinger, considers that Fatih Sultan Mehmed, who was exposed to fourteen assassination attempts, was finally poisoned in the fifteen attempt.

Doctors who gave that syrup to the Khan, The Khan drank the syrup thirstily,

The syrup ruined the liver of the Khan, his blood burned at that moment,

He said why the doctors sacrificed me, and colored my liver and life to blood . . .

And he used the statements of Ashiq Pashazada to support his thesis. The fact that the private doctor of Fatih Sultan Mehmed, Hekim Yakup Pasha, was torn to pieces by the Janissaries, fortified the possibility of assassination.

Maestro Jacopo was a Venetian doctor who converted to Islam. According to Babinger, the Republic of Venice promised Yakup Pasha a great fortune, accepted him and his posterity to the citizenship, and also exempted all of his descendants from the Republic's taxes.

But according to the chronicles of the Ottoman historians of that period as Kemal Pashazada, Dursun Bey, Ashiq Pashazada, and Hodja Sadaddin Effendi, the cause of death of Fatih Sultan Mehmed was gout, which was almost a genetic sickness of the members of the dynasty, and they didn't mention the claim of poisoning.

Kemal Pashazada indicates, "The sickness was preventing him from walking long distances. Gout was transmitted to him from his ancestors. In his last time he was seriously suffering from it."

Ashiq Pashazada explains the reason of his death as follows: "The reason for his death was the sickness that he had in his foot. The Doctors were incapable of curing it. Finally the doctors came together. And agreed. They took blood from his feet. The sickness rose. Then they gave him a relaxing syrup. Eventually he rejoined the Mercy of the most Merciful."

Dursun Bey the historian of Fatih's period explains the death of the sultan with the following words:

"While traveling to the other side and crossing the sea, his old sickness relapsed and sighed. His old sickness reappeared once the expedition was started. The imperial state tent was situated on the hayfield of *tekfur*. The weakness of his body reminded him that his time had come just like it reminds every faithful Muslim. The sultan, who fulfilled his reign with maturity, courage, and force all this time, left the worldly wealth and his sovereignty without staying separated from the judgment of Allah and his blessed spirit rejoined Allah."

Hodja Sadaddin Effendi also stated that Fatih, who passed to Üsküdar for the expedition, was feeling weak those days, but despite this he went on the expedition, after indicating that he stayed a couple of days in Üsküdar and hit the road to Gebze, Hodja Sadaddin Effendi explained how painful his death was, "The day they were situated in hayfield of Tekfur his state was pretty shattered, and his pain was considerably increased."

Mehmed Nashri Effendi describes the death of the sultan in his book *Kitab al-Jihannuma* (The Book Showing the Whole Word) as:

"In April 27, 1481, they passed to the other side and walked to Gebze without knowing the target of the expedition. After passing a couple of places, on Thursday, May 3, of the same year he traveled with horse-drawn vehicles and settled down to the hayfield of Maltepe close to Gebze. And they were saying that he was sick when they left Istanbul. The strangers weren't aware of his sickness as he traveled in a horse-drawn vehicle. In the afternoon of the day they settled to Maltepe, his spirit left his body as an angel and passed to the sacred realm and reached peace."

After analyzing all this information about the cause of death of Fatih Sultan Mehmed, we reach this conclusion: There is no sign or hint in the chronicles that were written between the fifteenth and sixteenth centuries by the Ottoman historians. The reason of his death was considered to be gout, which progressed after 1465. It is indicated that after all the effort of the doctors, he couldn't be saved. But the Austrian historian Franz Babinger did not have the same conviction. In the book that he wrote by also scanning the western sources, *Mehmed the Conqueror and His Time*, he came up with the argument that is still discussed that, "We are not sure of the cause of death of Mehmed. The fact that he had a lot of enemies and some of the details shows us that he was probably poisoned." Some of our modern historians, especially the deceased Yılmaz Öztuna, came up with this thesis constantly in various writings and books that he wrote and prepared the ground to raise its fame.

AN OVERVIEW ON FATIH'S PERIOD

When Fatih Sultan Mehmed ascended to the throne, the crisis of the Interregnum Period were overcome and the previous borders before the Battle of Ankara were approximately reached. The Ottoman State was substantially settled in the area between the Danube River in the Balkans and the Euphrates River in the Eastern Anatolia. The acreage of the Ottoman country after the conquest of Istanbul when it is calculated with the vassal countries was approximately 964,000 km². Nearly half of this land was in Anatolia and the other half was in Rumelia. The acreage of the empire at the death of Fatih also with the vassal countries reached to 2,214,000 km². Three quarters of the land was from the Balkans, and the empire seemed to be almost a European state. The conquest of Rumelia, Serbia, Mora, Wallachia, Bosnia, Herzegovina, Albania, and Bogdan changed also the demographic structure of the state and the non-Muslim population became higher than the Muslim population.

The new system that was established by the Ottomans after the conquests in Rumelia was welcomed with rejoicing by the peasants and the locals. The lands that were belonging to seigneurs and noble classes in the conquered countries were changed to be Ottoman property, and the heavy taxes and drudgery were removed. Removing drudgeries and settling a fair tax system led the Balkan nations to adopt Ottoman dominance and made it sympathetic. Also the Balkan Christians who were Orthodox were taken under the protection of the Ottomans after reviving the Greek Orthodox Patriarchate once Istanbul was conquered. This means that the Ottoman State obtained the status of political and religious protector of the Orthodox Balkan Christians. So the Orthodox who were defeated from Catholic pressure and the Italian exploitation achieved an economical increase too. Accordingly, Fatih, who assured the separation of the Orthodox and Catholics, prevented a massive unification of a Christian Crusade.

The declarations of Daniel Goffman about the issue are very informative:

"The regimes, which were removed by the Ottomans, were already not legitimate and they had a very bad reputation. The fourth Crusade in 1204 didn't only bring deviant administrators to most of those Greek Orthodox lands just because they were Catholics. But those Catholic administrators also exploited their vassals with high taxes and drudgery. The Byzantine emperors also were part of similar exploitations. The rage of Greek Orthodox Christians to the Catholic regimes facilitated the work of the Ottoman State where non-Muslims were enriched. The Ottomans didn't prefer the narrow-mindedness of the Catholic and Orthodox world. Instead of that they established a society where non-Muslims could live in relative freedom by benefiting from the equality of Central Asia, their participatory traditions and tolerance of Islam. The people who were oppressed by the exclusionist Christian states found this alternative much more attractive."

When the manuscripts from XV century are analyzed, it is understood that the Orthodox public of the period considered the conqueror of Istanbul entitled to the throne of the Byzantine Empire and embraced him as a ruler:

"This text was written in the period of the reign of our great chief Mehmed Bey."

"This text was written in the twenty-second year of the glorious sovereignty of the magnificent Muslim tsar Mehmed Bey. The Turks seized Shkoder this year."

"And this text was written in the days of the sovereignty of the magnificent Muslim tsar Mehmed Bey. This year Tsar Mehmed fought Uzun Hasan, with this battle entering the land that is under the sovereignty of our ruler."

The famous Roman historian Nicolae Jorga transmits from a Serbian Janissary:

"The Turks are righteous to themselves, to the other citizens without any religious distinction and to the vassal countries. The Ottoman officers travel the country four times a year in order to control the population. The *qadi* judges according to the Muslim law only when there is a disagreement between Muslims. Requesters can consult headmen, priests and even metropolitans whenever they want. Who attempt to exploit the poor population are those who get the severest punishment. Even stealing a chicken from a villager may put life at risk."

The general overview by Nicolae Jorga about Fatih Sultan Mehmed and his period is:

". . . Just like the ancient Rome period peace was dominant in the new empire. Pax Romana was established again and everyone was happy about it. When we compare the Polish and Hungarian traditions which forced their villagers and other citizens to suffer despite all the promises, the system of the little Slav states that brought discomfort, the heavy oppressions of the Byzantine seniors who exploit their citizens constantly and the chaos in Germany of the Emperor Frederich who thinks only about his interest, the countries of the Ottoman State displayed a peaceful and open contrast. Nobody needed to be afraid because of his religion or race. The habits and traditions were untouchable."

If we categorize the expeditions of Fatih Sultan Mehmed to the Balkans according to their military, economical, and political objectives we can say that:

Amasra, Sinop, Trabzon were conquered, the land of the Karamanlides was seized and the Ak Koyunlu army, which represented a serious threat, was heavily defeated in Otlukbeli in order to establish a political unification in Anatolia.

The southern coast of the Black Sea, Amasra, Sinop, and Trabzon were conquered, Crimea in the northern Black Sea, and Bogdan in the western Black Sea were seized in order to dominate the Black Sea and control the trade routes of the Black Sea.

The Aegean islands and Ionian islands of the Adriatic were conquered, and the Italian military landing was realized to dominate the Aegean and Mediterranean Sea. The empire's navy forces, which were weak before, were empowered after the expeditions that were organized to the Black Sea, Aegean and the Adriatic, and the state obtained a seafaring identity.

Fatih Sultan Mehmed is the real founder of the Ottoman navy. The Ottomans, who had approximately thirty galleys in 1451, had two hundred and fifty warships and approximately five hundred transplant ships in 1481. F. Babinger describes this great progress as "astonishing," and indicates that the Ottoman navy became superior to the European navy.

The gunnery technology also realized a splendid progress in Fatih's period. The spread of modern gunnery from the Ottomans to Europe prepared the end of a feudal system of thousand years. In reality the primitive cannons were first used in the battles of Europe from the fourteenth century. For example the British used one of those cannons against the French in the Battles of Kresy

(August 26, 1346) during the Hundred Years' Wars (1337–1453). The Ottomans' first cannon attempt was in the War of Kosovo in 1389. The objective of the usage of those primitive cannons was more to create an atmosphere of fear and panic for the enemy and appall the horses. But Fatih destroyed the city walls of Istanbul and used the big cannons in order to demolish the enemy's army. The cannon called "şahi" had an unprecedented effect and was a result of extremely superior engineering knowledge. Also "Mortar with vertical projectile direction," which was used during a siege, was a first. Also, explosive cannons were poured in order to be used on the battlefield. In the expeditions that were organized to besiege the fortresses on high cliffs of Albania, the equipment was brought to the region of the siege and the cannons were poured there quickly. These events that were narrated also by Kritovulos show the level reached by the Ottomans in artillery.

The Turks transformed the cannons into an effective tool of siege and war, which proved that big ramparts, forts, and castles can be destroyed. After that progress, it didn't took long for the European kings to bring the seigniors and overlords to their knees, and gather all their lands under the central power. From the sixteenth century, the central kingdoms and monarchies grew stronger while the seigniors were defeated against the kings and lost their lands. The political regimes of the European countries changed; the state took the place of the feudal system.

The Ottomans influenced the start of geographical discoveries, which changed the course of world history. Because after Istanbul and the Black Sea were subdued by the Turks, the Ottomans obtained a voice on the control of the Silk Roads and Spice Routes, and the European states became dependent on the Turks in term of commerce. The European kings, who were stalemated by the conquests of the Ottoman navy in the Adriatic and the Aegean Sea, started to research new ways to reach India and the Far East for new trade routes which led to the geographical discoveries.

Sultan Mehmed, who is one of the greatest statesmen, worked all his life to achieve the objective of transforming the Ottoman State to a real empire. He attempted conquests and realized deep organizational operations in this direction. According to Halil İnalcık, "Fatih gathered two very important characteristics of the empire builders of the history: A powerful leader who runs after world domination and a powerful man with a wide horizon. The ideal of transforming his state to the most powerful and superior empire of the world overtook all the acts of this great sultan."

Fatih Sultan Mehmed was not only a high-level marshal, but also he was a talented diplomat. During his sultanate sometimes he had to fight with four or five states at the same time, and found himself besieged by his enemies from the east and west. In those kind of critical periods he managed to achieve his aim in any case, sometimes by compromising his enemies, sometimes by delaying them, sometimes by dividing them from each other.

Osman Bey settled a principality of Kayı Tribe, and Orhan and Murad Bey transformed this principality to a state with the organizational activities they led. Fatih Sultan Mehmed moved the Ottoman state forward to an empire and wanted to make Istanbul the center of the Mediterranean. This ambidextrous sultan, who established a very powerful centralized structure in his state management, succeeded in gathering Anatolia, Rumelia, the Balkans, the Black Sea, and the Aegean in a state integrity centralized in Istanbul.

Sultan Mehmed, who made great effort to establish a modern central imperial, first sent away the aristocrat Turk families that limited the authority of the sultan from important state positions and relied on the ultimate obedience of the Devşirme statesman who took their places. In that period the Turkish aristocracy received a severe blow while the dominance of the Devşirme started in the empire. In fact after the death of Fatih, the Devşirmes supported Bayezid while the Turkmens supported Cem in the struggle of power and the Devşirmes were victorious in this struggle. In the beginning of his sultanate he dismissed Çandarlı Halil Pasha who was the leader of the Turkish aristocracy and mostly worked with Devşirme grand viziers in the following years.

The most successful grand vizier who was assigned by Fatih Sultan Mehmed, Mahmut Pasha was the son of a Byzantine Roman father and a Serbian mother. Mahmut Pasha was captured by the Akıncıs around Smederevo in 1427 and he was sold to Mehmed Agha, and after his intelligence was noticed he was given to Murad II. After he studied in Enderun School for a while he was given to serve the grand vizier Mehmed. Mahmut Pasha's brother Michael Angelovic was a member of one of the most important families of Serbia; he was one of the prominent statesmen of the Serb despot and he was almost leading the Turkish lobby that was working for the Ottomans to conquer Serbia. He was also the cousin of the philosopher Georgios Amiroutz, who was the government spokesman of David Komnenos, the emperor of the Empire of Trebizond. Mahmut Pasha achieved serious success during his first period as grand vizier from 1455 to 1467, and was chosen as a grand vizier again in 1472. But after some of the statesmen provoked Fatih against him he was dismissed from his position and was executed. His execution caused deep sadness in the scientific and artistic milieu, and it is because of love from the public that he was titled as "veli" (saint). The Western references describe and praise him as "the most brave and erudite man of the palace." And it is also indicated that Pasha was consulted even after he was dismissed from his position as grand vizier.

Mehmed Pasha, who was another grand vizier of Fatih, was of the Byzantine Roman descent and for that reason he was famed as "Rum Mehmed Pasha" among the people. He served between 1467 and 1470 but he didn't have a good reputation among the public. One of the historians who lived in that period, Ashiq Pashazada, describes that the sultan ordered to "choke him as a dog" because of his maltreatment of the people and especially the Turks. One of the important grand viziers of the period is the conqueror of Italy, Gedik Ahmed Pasha. He was the son-in-law of Ishak Pasha, who was one of the Turk grand viziers of Fatih. Ahmed Pasha was trained in the Janissary Organization and was of Serbian or Albanian origin. He served as a grand vizier between 1474 and 1477, and he made serious contributions to the seizing of Crimean land in 1475. The Turk grand viziers of Fatih Sultan Mehmed's period are Çandarlı Halil Pasha, Ishak Pasha, and Karamani Mehmed Pasha.

Some of the navy commanders of Fatih's period were Mesih Pasha who was grand vizier in Bayezid II period and the brave commander Has Murad Pasha who was martyred in the Battle of Otlukbeli, both of whom were also of the Byzantine Roman descent. Zağanos Pasha, who was always with Fatih in the beginning of his sultanate against the team of Çandarlı Halil Pasha and also supported him until the end of the conquest of Istanbul, was of Albanian descent. Another Rumelia governor, Hadım Suleiman Pasha, was Bosnian. The famous grand vizier of Yavuz Sultan Selim period, Hersekzade Ahmed Pasha was the son of Stephan, the duke of Bosnia, and he was raised in the Ottoman palace during Fatih's period. The Admiral Baltaoğlu Suleiman Bey, who was dismissed after his failure against the Romans during the siege of Istanbul, was a Bulgarian nobleman.

Fatih raised his ultimate authority over the high-level administrative positions by assigning the Devşirmes, and he also adjusted the Kapıkulu army and reorganized it in order to obligate it to ultimate obedience. He also adjusted the salary of the Kapıkulu army, which was formed by the choicest soldiers, and renewed their arms and equipment constantly. The Kapıkulu army was going to be the unique support of Fatih Sultan Mehmed in his intense expedition attempts. He also cut out the Akıncı margraves, who were acting almost independently for power struggles in the following years of the Ottoman Interregnum by establishing the "veteran ruler" identity. There wasn't a similar example of the centralized state model that was established by Fatih Sultan Mehmed in Europe at that period. The first example of centralized empire that were going to increase in the New Age was the Ottoman state, which was established in Fatih's period.

His basic objective was concentrated on the idea of "ruling the world as an ultimate empire." Jakopo Languschi who was situated in Istanbul after its conquest wrote that the objective of the sultan was to establish one empire, one faith, and one ruler in the world. Ibn Kemal pointed Fatih's idea of dominating the world by stating "dominating the world was in his mind." Accordingly he internalized being the representative of the holy war in the Islamic world and the protector of Islamic countries.

The performance displayed by the Ottomans against the Crusade, the battles that they won, the achieved conquests and the spread of Islam in the Balkan geography led the Islamic world to great joy. For example, according to Ibn Ayas; the celebrations that were made in Cairo after the conquest of Istanbul lasted for days. A *mehter* squad gave concerts to the public, prayers were fulfilled in the mosques with the command of the Abbasid caliph, and the Mamluk sultan sent messengers to Fatih in order to congratulate him on the conquest of Constantinople. The conquest of Constantinople, which was the capital of the Roman Empire, and the last castle of Christianity in the east by the Ottomans led to deep turbulences in Europe. The important historian of the French Academy, Rene Groesset, explains the Conquest of Istanbul and the East-West relations from a wide perspective after his profound analyzes as: ". . . The progression of the Ottoman Turks from Bursa to Vienna ended in 1912 with the withdrawal to Edirne. Finally the Ottomans succeeded in conquering Rome. Because they had great rulers who came one after the other. Those rulers had an incomparable military intelligence. They knew what they wanted and they didn't have other objectives than conquest. The descendant of Osman revived the sacred ideals of their Prophet's expeditions."

Fatih Sultan Mehmed wasn't claiming to be only an Ottoman ruler. He was considering himself as the successor of the Roman Empires too. The Cretan scholar Georgios Trapezuntios said to Fatih in 1466, "No doubt that you are the emperor of Rome. Who seizes the throne city is legally the emperor. And the throne city in the Roman Empire is Istanbul." Trapezuntios lived between 1395 and 1484, and he died when he was eighty-nine in Rome; he was fifty-eight during the conquest and seventy-one when he told those words, he was a mature man who knew what he was saying. Trapezuntios was claiming that "Fatih was greater than Cyrus, the Great Alexander and Caesar and the other rulers that came and past." Also according to him, "Fatih didn't terminate the Roman Empire. The empire continues as Muslim as it did before as Pagan, Christian, and Orthodox. We can claim that by the routes of conquests and the acts."

Western Rome was the next after seizing the Eastern Roman Empire but the sudden death of Fatih Sultan Mehmed prevented this big project. This ideal was hold on by his successors. Of course the changing circumstances and the conjuncture had also an effect on this.

There were Italian and Byzantine courtiers among the Muslim ones in the Ottoman palace during Fatih's period. The sultan analyzed the Renaissance culture and the Roman history from those consultants. According to Paul Faure, who has done important studies about the Renaissance, the Renaissance started in 1453 with the conquest of Istanbul. Fatih, who was idealized as the ideal type of ruler of the Renaissance, was not only praised and glorified in Europe but also in Russia.

Akdes Nimet Kurat is a Russian History expert, and he states in his book called *Russian History*, "The Russian writer Perevetov described Fatih as an exemplar philosopher, politician, and military man in his book called *About Sultan Mehmed* that he presented to Tsar Ivan IV." From 1594 to 1749, six pieces about Fatih were written in England.

The Byzantine historian Kritovulos stated while he presented his book to Fatih, "To Mehmed the greatest emperor, the ruler of rulers, the master of the land and seas, unbeatable, the victorious with Allah's Will." Françesco Berlinghieri and Roberto Balturia are among the Roman writers who presented their works to Fatih. Also, Stefano Emiliano wrote a lamentation about the death of the sultan. The most famous poem that was presented to Fatih was the poem of 4706 verses written by Giovanni Maria Fielfo. The Italian poets were saluting and indicating the need of a powerful leader who was going to unify Italy that was known by its fragmented political system in poems such as that one.

The expenses of the empire seriously rose in Fatih's period. Reconstructing Istanbul, which was conquered, the expenses that were spent for urbanization and civil service reached great amounts. At the same time, the expeditions and wars that were realized in thirty years by an extremely energetic and weariless sultan raised the expenses to extreme levels. The expenses considerably rose with augmenting the number of soldiers to protect the seized castles, the number of the Janissaries, the raise that was applied to the soldiers' salaries, the constant renovation of arms and equipment needed for battles.

The sultan, who was obliged to find new sources of income, didn't regret using state and public financial possibilities as much as possible, and he took radical precautions in this direction. Those tough precautions led to a deep disapproval among the public.

Fatih Sultan Mehmed in Levni's depiction

During his sultanate, each five years he used to gather the current coins and change them with new ones after reducing a fifth, thus he imposed some sort of tax. He provided a great income to the treasury by establishing monopolies on essential necessities like soap, salt, and candles. He canceled the land registrations of demesnes, which became foundation land and transformed them back to demesnes. He gave those lands as timars, aiming to raise the number of cavalrymen. The real estate was considered as state-owned after the conquest, and even though those lands were given to the villagers in order to encourage migration to Istanbul, later they we charged *muqata'a*, which means rent.

Those radical precautions which empowered the central treasury led to dissatisfaction among the public, scholars, Sufis, and traders. Because of this dissatisfaction the public and the statesmen didn't support Cem, who was the follower of his father's policies, but they supported his other son Bayezid in the struggle for the throne after the death of Fatih Sultan Mehmed.

KANUNNAME-I AL-I OSMAN
(THE OTTOMAN CODE OF LAWS)

The period of Fatih Sultan Mehmed is extremely important for the improvement of the law understanding in the Ottoman state. Fatih wanted to have the ultimate domination by establishing the centralized empire through state organizations and law regulations. *Kanunname-i Al-i Osman* was prepared with the command of Fatih and can be considered as the first Ottoman codex and was written by Nishanji Leyszada Mehmed Effendi in the grand viziership of Karamani Mehmed Pasha. "This code of laws is the law of my ancestor and my grandfather. And it is my law too." We understand in this statement that those judgments that were preached in various epochs and were included in the Imperial Council were reconsidered and accomplished. Fatih's code of laws had vital importance for the organization of the Ottoman state and the history of its state organization, and it was integral to state institutions for centuries.

Fatih's code of laws is made up of three sections:

1. The position of the central and village state officers in the protocol,

2. The organization of state and sultanate tasks,

3. Crimes, punishments and the income of statesmen,

Those texts that were used as an official state code in Fatih's period, enlighten the understanding of the law of the Ottoman state, and are extremely precious sources that represent its political, social, cultural, and economic character. Sultan Mehmed, who internalized a flexible understanding of the law, indicated the possibility of regulating them according to need by saying, "Regulation about various circumstances are established. My gracious descendants who will come after me should work on reforming it."

The code of laws

FROM PRINCE MEHMED TO
FATIH SULTAN MEHMED

ehmed II who was the seventh sultan of the Ottoman State, was born in Edirne 1432 as the fourth
son of Murad II from Hüma Hatun. Murad II paid
special attention to the education of the prince, who was
extremely intelligent, energetic, and combative. He took
lessons from the greatest scholars of the period in Edirne
Palace. His first teacher was Molla Yegan; later he was
presented to Aq Shams al-Din, with the authorization
that he would be beaten when it was necessary for his
education.

When he was eleven years old, Prince Mehmed was
sent to Manisa as a flag officer with his tutor Kasabzade
Mahmut, his teachers and consultants, and with the sudden death of his older brother Alaeddin Ali Çelebi in
the same year, he became the heritor of the Ottoman
throne. After his father abdicated in 1444 he became sultan when he was only twelve years old. In 1446 Murad II
took back his position and he was sent again to Manisa
as a flag officer. In this period, which was going to last till

1451, he was busy with increasing his state experience, knowledge, and background.

Prince Mehmed got to know the Greek and Roman culture in that period. The Prince, who gathered some of the Italian humanists, and various foreign intellectuals from Genoa, Venice, and Napoli, was working on learning Greek and Latin. He made his teacher of Latin and Italian, Cyriacus, who was considered as the founder of modern archeology, read him Roman and European history every night. From the time he was prince till the end of his life he kept Byzantine, Arab, Persian, and Turkish scholars and also Western humanists among his immediate surroundings and always kept in touch with them.

Istanbul lost its liveliness and became unproductive from all aspects including science and culture in 1204 after the Roman invasion and was revitalized again with cultural enterprises after it was seized by the Ottomans. Fatih Sultan Mehmed wanted to transform Istanbul to a world capital of knowledge, culture, and tolerance, and he started to construct the empire from Istanbul.

In the period of Fatih the city was adorned with scientific, cultural, and religious monuments. After the conquest he transformed eight churches to schools, and designated competent scholars, Mawlana Tusi, Hodjazada, and Mawlana Abdülkerim to those schools as chief teachers. Fatih Mosque is the first big mosque of Istanbul, and four schools were constructed in the north and four others in the south of it. Nineteen rooms were added to each section of the *Sahn-ı Seman* Schools that were constructed as eight faculties, and also seventy rooms were appropriated for a *darüşşifa* (hospital), which was working on a practical level. The Sultan was paying special attention to the students who were studying in the *Sahn-ı Seman* Schools, and he attended the lessons from time to time, and was informed about their assignations and advancements. The *Sahn-ı Seman* Schools were concentrating specially on medicine, law, and theology; they were one of the big cultural centers of the period and also the basis of Istanbul University is attributed to those schools and the founding date of the university is considered to be 1453.

In addition to those schools, the sultan established two preparatory schools around Hagia Sophia Mosque and Eyüp Sultan Mosque. He also ordered his viziers to construct mosques, commercial centers, and schools in order to liven up Istanbul. Mahmut Pasha, Davut Pasha, and Mustafa Pasha constructed schools in different districts of the city. He was aware that the first condition of a world empire is a strong system of education, and he organized the educational, religious, and law institutions and rearranged the curriculum of the schools in Istanbul, Edirne, and Bursa.

Sciences such as Islamic Law, Islamic Theology, and Qur'anic Exegesis have been taught according to the classical techniques in the Ottoman schools until the Fatih Sultan Mehmed period. A particular attention was paid to classical science and positive science, and philosophical and scientific ideas were supported and encouraged in his period. The Sultan protected all the scientists without any religious, racial, or denominational discrimination, and progress was made in all areas owing to this positive atmosphere.

The Austrian Ottoman historian Paul Wittek says, "The protection of the magnificent church Hagia Sophia and its resistance to the years passing is a result of the superior engineering knowledge of the Turks. The victorious Turks had a high civilization where the Islamic world found perfection and after the conquest they developed a new move for this civilization. Sultan Mehmed constructed a new mosque, which competes Hagia Sophia and a new complex that consists of eight schools, hospitals, and a library, he also constructed a new university which attracted the scholars of the Islamic world. Constructing the city was going to be progressed by his successors and the spectacular Istanbul was going to shape the future of Asia and Europe."

The German historian Mordtmann describes Fatih as, "He was a milestone for world history, and he gathered the culture of both worlds in his personality." He tried to gather the distinguished scholars of rational and traditional science as if he was willing to synthesize Western culture with Eastern culture. We can analyze the vision, world view, and intellectual personality of the

Sultan by studying his relationships with Eastern scholars and Western philosophers:

Gennadios Skholarios was giving lectures to Greek and Italian students in the academy that he established in his house before the conquest, and he was strongly opposing the idea of the Emperor Constantine regarding unifying with the Catholic Church. In fact, the Greek Cardinal Isidoros declared the unification of the Catholic and Orthodox churches on December 12, 1452, after a Rome-style ritual, and Gennadios strongly disaffirmed this act. His brave reaction and polemics with Isidoros raised his respect among the Orthodox public. Fatih Sultan Mehmed ordered that Gennadios, who was captured in Edirne after it was seized, be brought to Istanbul. He hadn't the needed qualifications to be chosen as patriarch according to the conventions of the church. After raising his spiritual level he was appointed to the Church of the Holy Apostles, which is the highest spiritual level, and in 1454 he was assigned as the chief patriarch of the Christian Orthodox Church. With this step Fatih clearly showed that he was on the side of the Orthodox; the aim was to deepen the divergence between the Catholics and the Orthodox. With this policy the Ottomans prevented the unification of the Christians and the Crusade attempts, and they established a lasting and easy domination particularly on the Orthodox from the Balkans.

Fatih respected the knowledge of Gennadios, who was an honest and frank theologian, and they were often having scientific conversations. The Sultan asked him to prepare a book that included the basic creeds of Christianity, so Gennadios wrote İtikatname, where he compiled the basic knowledge about Christianity and presented it to the Sultan. He also arranged a discussion in his presence between Muslim scholars and the Patriarch Maxim Manuel about Christian faith and demanded to transcribe this discussion from the patriarch.

The Pope Pius (1458–1464) wasn't able to understand the intellectual and political research of Fatih and his dialogues with Christian philosophers; he thought that the sultan was inclined to Christianity and he wrote him a long letter in 1461. The Pope's letter was published under the title "Epistola ad Mahometem" in 1469 Italy, and says:

"However this little and unimportant thing will make you the greatest, most powerful, and most famous person. If you ask me what it is. It is not hard to find it out. No need for deep research. A handful of water that is needed for your baptism can be found anywhere in the world. Turn to the Christian rituals and believe in the Bible. Do that. There won't be any equivalent ruler in the world to you in terms of grandeur, greatness, and power. We promise you: We will entitle you as the emperor of the Greeks and the East. The lands that you seized by force will be your merit. It is impossible for you to be successful with Islamic law. But if you turn to Christianity you will be the greatest man of our epoch."

The original copy of the letter is kept in Vatican archives. This letter never reached the sultan for unknown reasons. Also any positive or negative reply was not encountered to this letter in any archive.

Silvio Piccolomini, one of the important humanists of the fifteen century, wrote, "When the Pope was still the secretary of Graz before he was titled, Pius II wrote his thoughts about the fall of Istanbul: "The sword of the Turks is swinging on our heads. Until now the Italians were the owners of the universe. Now the empire of the Turks is starting. The Venetian Senate is in deep sorrow, because the Venetians may lose the right to sail not only in the Black Sea but also in Syria, Crete, and the Adriatic."

The Byzantine historian Kritoboulos, who foretold to one of his Byzantine friends in an early year like 1444, that no power would be able to stand against the Ottomans, was among those who entered Fatih's service. The sultan assigned him as the governor of Imbros Island in 1456. After his governance, which lasted for ten years, Kritoboulos left to Istanbul when the island was seized by the Venetians and became the official historian of Sultan Mehmed. In his book that he wrote about the activities of Fatih from 1451 to 1467, he indicates that "Sultan is one of the most brilliant philosophers." And tells that "he ordered to translate the *Lives of the Roman Emperors* of Plutarch from Greek to Turkish and he was particularly interested in Alexander and Julius Caesar's life stories."

Georgios Amirutzes was one of the important geographers and philosophers of the Byzantine Empire and was captured after the conquest but it became clear that he was a worthwhile scholar, he was assigned to the consultant staff of the sultan. But he was considered treacherous by his European co-religionists because of his intimate relationship with the sultan. Amirutzes who was the mathematical, philosophy, and geographical consultant of the sultan, translated "Almagest" of Ptolemy to Arabic upon the order of the sultan. One of his two sons became Muslim and took Mehmed as a name, and translated the Bible to Arabic upon the order of Fatih. Fatih also analyzed the world map of Ptolemy. A Latin translation of Ptolemy geography made by Jakobus Anglos was found in his library. Because of the geographic curiosity of the sultan Topkapı Palace was almost transformed into a geographical academy. The Ottoman sultan's particular interest in geography books and maps attracted some of the Italian printing houses. Berlinghieri came to Istanbul in order to sell the special print of Ptolemy's *Geographica*. But because of Fatih's death, he presented the book to Bayezid and he sold it to him by telling him that he prepared the book for his father and that he dedicated it to him. That wasn't enough for Berlinghieri; he also sold another book with a high copyright fee to Prince Cem, who was exiled in Europe.

Georgios Trapezountios was a child of a family that migrated from Trabzon to Crete, settled to Italy in 1416 and became Catholic in 1426; he attempted to translate Plato, Aristotle and Demosthenes; he was a worthwhile man who also taught some of the popes. In those years that humanism was popular, Trapezountios was hoping that the dream of the unification of humanity under one power could be realized only by a Turkish ruler. Although he came to Istanbul as the representative of Pope Paul II in 1465, he couldn't meet the Sultan. When he came back, he wrote a text called "About the Majesty of the Sultan." He was imprisoned by the Cardinal of Trabzon Bessarion because of his writing about Fatih. Then he managed to get out the prison by apologizing to the pope and telling him that his praises to the sultan were in order to make him change his religion. In one of his writings Trapezountios says: "I think that the opportunity that God gave to your personage was not obtained by anyone and it will not be, I reached this conclusion after God granted you with Constantinople... God conveyed sovereignty to you with this victory. In order to gather all the people under one faith and one church and to glorify you as the ruler of the whole world."

The Italian painter Gentile Bellini was invited by the sultan and stayed in Istanbul from 1479 to 1480 where he accomplished the portrait of Fatih Sultan Mehmed and other paintings. Today the painting of Fatih Sultan Mehmed is exposed at the National Gallery of London. The Italian Angiolollo also writes that he met Bellini in the palace. The Venetian painter and medal maker from

Verona, Matteo D'Patsi was in Istanbul too but none of his works have been found. It is also estimated that the sultan collected information about the country of those artists that he invited. The adventure of Matteo D'Patsi can be considered as a typical example. D'Patsi was searched by the papal soldiers on the border and he was tried, charged with espionage, when the letter that was written to Fatih was found on him.

Sultan Mehmed took sons of Byzantine aristocrats to Enderun School after the conquest, and in the following years he assigned those individuals to state tasks. He assigned Mehmed and Mesih Pasha as grand vizierships; and Has Murad Pasha as governor. In other words the Byzantine scholars and politicians were embodied in the Ottoman culture and they were allowed to contribute to the social and political Ottoman life. This approach proves that the imperial vision was beginning to be established.

In the fifteenth century the scientific and intellectual level in the Ottoman Empire reached high levels because of the wise ruler who patronized all the scholars without ethnic or religious discrimination. This scientific dynamism that started in Fatih's period, the explosion in translating and writings, bore fruit after Fatih's period. Additionally new and original contributions to Islamic science were made in different scientific fields. Classical Islamic knowledge reached its highest limits especially in mathematics, astronomy, geography, and medicine. For example, in that period forty-three scientists wrote sixty-three books in the field of mathematics.

The sultan conquered Istanbul, which was the capital of the Roman Empire, and declared it as his capital, and besides that he wanted to make it the center of the Islamic world and the ancient world. For that reason he invited the scholars that he could reach with attractive offers to Istanbul. The assignation of Ali Qushji (d. 1474) as the chief teacher of Hagia Sophia School after transferring him from Tabriz is a good example.

Ali Qushji was called "Qushjizade" because his father was the falconer of the Timur State rulers, and he was raised in the palace of Uğur Bey, who was the wise ruler of the Timur Renaissance that shone as a sun on Asia. He took lessons from Qadizada and Jamshidi Kashi and other scholars of the palace. After the death of Qadizada he was assigned to the Observatory of Samarkand. He wrote unique books in the fields of astronomy and mathematics. The most important book of Ali Qushji was his commentary that he wrote to Zic-i Uluğ Bey. He presented proofs to Zic's theorems and problems. After Uluğ Bey was killed by his son Abdullatif in 1449, Qushji migrated to Tabriz, which was the capital of Ak Koyunlu State. He took his place among the committee that was sent by Uzun Hasan to Istanbul. Fatih Sultan Mehmed noticed the potential of Ali Qushji and he offered him to stay in Istanbul. Qushji accepted the offer after insistent persuasions, and he came to Istanbul with an expense of one hundred persons after fulfilling his legation duty. He was paid one thousand coins for each stop during his journey. After he settled in the capital he was assigned as the chief teacher of the Hagia Sophia with a salary of two hundred coins per day. The task of arranging the academic program of the Hagia Sophia and the *Sahn-ı Seman* Schools was also given to him. The lessons that he was giving in Hagia Sophia School reached a great amount of participants and attracted the attention of the attendees.

A mufti

Serious scientific progress was achieved in the Ottoman land with the students who were raised by the famous astronomer and mathematician Ali Qushji. He wrote sufficient books and raised hundreds of students. Fathullah Shirwani was another important astronomer and mathematician. They were among the last stars of the Timur Renaissance. Shirwani, who took lessons from Qadizada in Samarkand School, was included earlier in the Ottoman education system and he came to Anatolia in the period of Murad II. He raised students for a long time while he was teaching in the schools of Istanbul. He died in 1486. Those two scholars, who transmitted the knowledge of the West, were pioneers of mathematics and astronomy in the Ottoman land. They contributed to a new expansion formed by the synthesis of the East and West and established an intellectual vision in the Islamic world.

Sinan Pasha (d. 1486) was another worthwhile scholar in Istanbul in Fatih's period. He took lessons from outstanding scholars such as Molla Husraw, Molla Gürani, Hodjazada, and Molla Yagan. He came to the fore with his intelligence and talent, he raised to the diaconate of the *Sahn-ı Seman* and then to "Hace-i Sultani," which is the private professor of the sultan. He wrote various Arabic books in the field of philosophy, Islamic law and interpretation among mathematics and astronomy. He was assigned as a vizier in 1471 and then as grand vizier to Kubbealtı, which led the public to call him "Hodja Pasha" (Professor Pasha). It is narrated that Sinan Pasha felt it beneath him to attend the mathematic lessons of Ali

Qushji when he came to Istanbul and for that reason he sent his student Tokatlı Molla Lütfi to the lessons and learned from him. After he was arrested by the sultan because of this mistake, all of the other scholars spoke with a single voice and declared that they would burn their books and leave the country. With that Sinan Pasha was released and designated to Sivrihisar. This interesting situation shows us how the scholars of that period had a strong character and how they were respected by the sultan.

Hodjazada (d. 1488), the great scholar from Bursa, was professor, judge of the army, private professor of the sultan, and the judge of Istanbul, and he was dedicated enough to resign from all the state positions because they were preventing his scientific research. Hodjazada, who was always praised because of his teachings more than his posts and positions, was well known in Iran and Central Asia. Husayn Baykara sent a scholar with the messenger that he sent in order to congratulate the succeeding of Bayezid II to the throne, to take lessons from Hodjazada. He attended debates with most of the scholars of his period in the presence of the sultan and mostly he came out victorious. Molla Zayrak and Ali Qushji were some of them. The sultan, who had a particular interest in metaphysics, religions, and history of sects, arranged a debate about *Tawhid* (Divine Unity) between Hodjazada and Molla Zayrak in his presence and this debate lasted for seven days. The winner of this debate, which was arbitrated by Molla Husraw, was Hodjazada. According to

Adnan Adıvar, this attribute of Hodjazada reminds us the scholar type called "Doctores Universales" in Europe. Sultan Mehmed turned to Hodjazada who was teaching him law in an expedition and asked him "Aren't you afraid to argue with me?" Hodjazada answered him, "I am afraid as your citizen, but I am not as your professor. Although you are my sultan outside now you are my disciple."

The sultan was open minded and far from bigotry, and was often inviting scholars to his palace and arranging scientific debates. He demanded writings from scholars about difficult matters and analyzed them. He arranged thorough debates concerning religion and philosophy to scholars that he respected such as Hodjazada, Molla Gürani, Aq Shams al-Din, and Ali Qushji.

One of the scholars who Fatih was trying to bring to Istanbul was Molla Cami from Khorasan. When the sultan learned that the great scholar went on pilgrimage he ordered to the dependent lands to host him in the best way possible and he sent him a messenger for inviting him to Istanbul when he was in Damascus. Molla Cami praised Fatih in *İrşadiye Risalesi* (The Treatise of Guidance) that he wrote to thank him, and after the second invitation he took the road with a crowded cortege, but he learned that the sultan had died when he arrived to Konya and he returned back with great sorrow.

Also great doctors were raised in the period of Fatih Sultan Mehmed and serious progress was achieved with those doctors in the field of medicine. The most important doctor of Ottoman medical history was Şerafeddin Sabuncuoğlu (d. 1469) who gained fame in surgery. Şerafeddin wrote important books and also translated the great Andalusian scholar Zahrawi's *Jarrahiyat al-Hani-yya* into Turkish. In this book that he contributed to, he also explained the tools and techniques of surgical interventions with pictures, and this book is an important booklet for surgical education. He wrote *Mücerrebname* (The Document Proven by Experience) in 1468, in which he transmitted all his experiences and he explained the practical treatment methods. Sabuncuoğlu is considered as one of the pioneers of the experimental pharmacology and tested the medicine and the mixtures that he made on animals. For example, he gave an antidote to a cock that was bitten by a snake and the cock survived.

Altunizade was the most famous expert of urologic diseases of his time. The book that was written by Aq Shams al-Din who was one of the professors of Fatih, *Maidat'ul-Hayat* (The Feast of Life), includes ideas that associate microbes and contamination. Hekim Arap, Hoca Ataullah, Herim Lari, and Yakup Pasha can be also considered as the famous doctors of that period.

Yakup Pasha was an Italian Jew who migrated to the Ottoman land after the Pope Nicola V excommunicated and dismissed the professional privileges of the Arabs and Jews who were living in Italy. He became the chief doctor after converting to Islam and was also the private doctor of Fatih. He was considered as the responsible for the death of Fatih and he was killed by the Janissaries.

Fatih Sultan Mehmed included Greek and Latin books in his library in Topkapı Palace among the Arabic, Persian, and Turkish books. Those books are kept today in the Topkapı Palace museum. It is known that he contributed approximately eight hundred books to the Hagia Sophia, the *Sahn-ı Seman* Schools, and his own library. According to the research made by the Professor of Berlin University, Adolf Deismann, there are 585 non-Islamic books in Fatih's library. Also 185 Greek manuscripts were sold in 1685 from the palace library.

Sultan Mehmed was writing poems with the nickname Avni and he was the first Ottoman Sultan who wrote a "divan." He always supported and protected cultural and scientific activities, and he also researched and banned the situations that impeded cultural movement. This event transmitted by Hammer is a good example:

"One day the sultan was talking to a mullah about how Crimea was a prosperous city and how it has various scholars who were always busy with writing. The mullah replied to him that this situation was in the past and that the new vizier treated the scholars badly and that he transformed Crimea, which had been like a paradise, into hell. The sultan told this situation to the grand vizier Mahmut Pasha and reminded him how to treat the intellectuals again."

Fatih was joking with scholars and dervishes and tolerated their weird behaviors as long as they didn't commit an obvious mistake. In one of the days that the sultan was incognito walking around, one of the dervishes recognized him and told him, "God Almighty created one hundred twenty-four prophets. For the love of each prophet give me one coin." The sultan smiled to the hard demand of the dervish and told him, "Tell me the name of each one of those prophets and I will give you the coins." How could this dervish know the name of all those prophets? He told him only a few names and the sultan avoided paying this high amount.

It is narrated that the statesmen and the viziers were wary to be in the presence of the sultan when scientific issues were debated, and scholars used to confabulate with the sultan intimately. This privileged treatment of the sultan to scholars pushed the statesmen to pay respect to them too, and protect them in order to support their scientific activities.

The sultan was enjoying being part of the intellectual milieu when he was in the capital, and he used to walk around with a pointy cotton cap bandaged with wide and plicate gauze.

Fatih was a far from bigotry; rather, he was an open minded, tolerant religious Muslim who had never enough of making jihad in the Name of Allah during his whole life. Carretto, who is the writer of "The Turks in Mediterranean," which presents a good analysis of the Ottoman

Turk history, states that, "Mehmed was a good Muslim although he had interest in the Western culture." Fatih Sultan Mehmed was also writing qualitative poems with clear statements comparing to his period.

My intent is to fight in the Name of Allah,

My effort is the unique effort of the religion of Islam . . .

His verses might give us an idea about his world view. The sultan was paying an extreme attention to applying the commandments and prohibitions of Islam, and he stated in an edict that he sent to the Greek provinces about paying attention to the prayers:

"May Allah the Almighty predestinate us to fulfill His orders. What I wanted to indicate in this statement is that: The Muslim community that lives in the cities, towns, and villages of the Greek land are opposing and showing weakness in adapting to the orders of the Islamic religion, the Prophetic Tradition, and the Holy Quran. They are not obeying the order of Allah '*Establish the Prayer in conformity with its conditions!*' and the *Hadith* 'Prayer is the basis of the religion. Who fulfills it conforming to its conditions fulfills the religion and who leaves it ruins the religion.' And they deviate to the path of rebellion, so the mosques are turned to ruin and waste, and they construct places of impiety and disobedience. We are getting similar information. If that's true ordering good and forbidding evil is incumbent upon me, I charged one of my qualified men for this task. He will analyze and examine this issue.

"I ordered that: Whoever abandons the prayer should be beaten and his assets should be condemned according to the orders of the Islamic religion for that the people who will be determined that they abandoned prayer in the Greek land will be punished. Prayer should be recommended to the public and who doesn't pray should be affronted and exposed. No one ever can prevent this operation! The seigniors and governors of the Greek land and those who are under their command should collaborate with the officer that I am sending. The weakness in fulfilling the orders of the Islamic religion will not be tolerated. So the mosques will be filled and the schools will be constructed and the Islamic religion will be empowered. Thus the Muslims will reach peace, prosperity, and happiness, and they will pray for the lasting of the republic and the power of their sultan. Let everyone know that. And trust my honorable sign."

WHAT DID THEY SAY ABOUT
FATIH SULTAN MEHMED?

Isodoros, the archpriest of Saint Demetrios Monastery, settled down in Italy in 1439, and in 1452 he came to Constantinople as the charged cardinal of the Vatican. He declared that the churches were unified after a Catholic ceremonial, and he was in the city during the siege and was responsible for defending the neighborhood of Saint Demetrios. He was wounded on his head with an arrow, and captured, but he managed to hide his identity although he was wanted and he escaped with a ransom. He reached Venice with a Turkish boat through Phocaea-Chios-Heraklion. Isidoros, who experienced the siege in detail and got to know Fatih, said, "He was reading Alexander's life every day from different books. He wanted to rule the world more than Alexander and Caesar." He warned the Pope by telling him, "Holy Father! He is threatening Christianity, he will conquer your city Rome in a soon by using power and arms."

The Podovian jurist Dotti, who was exiled to Crete because his involvement in an assassination in 1438, reached the conviction after listening the Greeks who experienced the war and went to the island that: "This awesome man is a second Alexander who has an extraordinary volition and great power."

Micheal Doukas who was sent to Fatih as a messenger in 1455, found the chance to have extensive speeches with the Janissaries, writes in his book where he explains the Ottoman-Byzantine relations that, "The unique concern of Sultan Mehmed during his days and night, whether he is sleeping or awake, in the palace or outside was with what kind of war and application he can conquer Constantinople . . ." and "The Byzantines gave rein Istanbul to the Ottomans as a punishment from God."

The close friend of Pope Pius II, Venice's messenger of Siena and the outspoken defender of the Crusades that was organized against the Turks Benvoglienti said that; "Mehmed is more powerful than Cesar, Alexander and all the other rulers who tried to rule the world."

Sekoundinos was captured with his family by the Turks for three months when Salonika was conquered in 1430, and then he worked as a translator in Euboea and later in Florence. Babinger considers his writings as the first European essays written about the roots of the Turks and the Ottoman history. Sekoundinos describes Fatih to us:

"Mahumettus has a great and acute intelligence. He showed his governance talents and palace knowledge in a short time after he took the place of his father; he dismissed whatever was unnecessary and unhelpful. He is not into hunting, birds, dance, singing, or feasts, and he is not lazy at all. He is always busy with something, always in motion; he doesn't run but almost flies. He thinks and whatever he decides he pays extreme attention in applying it. Bad weather doesn't prevent him, cold, hunger, and thirst doesn't affect him. He deals with literature and philosophy while he is busy with governance. He has very wise philosophers in his entourage. He talks with them in a friendly way and analyzes the history with their guidance. He isn't interested only in Sparta and Athens but also the history of Rome and Carthage. He likes to study the actions of Alexander and Caesar."

Zorzo Dolfin, who was twenty-one years old during the conquest of Istanbul, describes the sultan with those words:

"He laughs little, he is very generous and his mind is always working. He is resistant to cold, hot, hunger, and thirst. He is stubborn, extremely venturesome and pretty daring concerning his projects. He is like the great Alexander who had never enough of honor and glory. He speaks precisely without hesitating. He refrains from pleasure and enjoyment. He speaks Turkish, Greek, and Serbian. He is extremely ambitious in any subject. He definitely reads every day for a while. He reads the history of the Roman Empire, Laerce, Herodotos, Tite-Live, Quinte Curse, the Papal State, Germany, France, and Lombardi's kings. He knows the Italian history with all its details, and knows the republics of Europe. He carries a big map of Europe with him. He always wants to domineer. He is proficient in adopting his state to the different conditions of various countries."

The Italian Langusto is also a coeval of Fatih, and he describes the sultan shortly after the conquest of Istanbul as:

"He has a thin face, he is tall with a noble attitude, he has a great heart, he instills fear more than respect, he smiles rarely, he is prudent, he has a profound will of learning, he is stubborn about his objectives, he is sure about himself in every subject, he is also talented in using arms and he seeks a fame that is not less than Alexander's fame. He makes Ciriaco or another Italian reads Roman history every night. His most favorite thing was the art of war. He is a smart researcher who wants to learn everything. He is self-denial and not into riotous living. He is resistant to all kind of hardship. He believes in establishing one empire and one sultanate in the world and he is convinced that there is not a better city than Istanbul to establish this union."

Soemmern, who had access to important documents and persons because of his critical position in the palace of the papacy, presents precious information about the Ottomans and Fatih and says, "He will seize Rome too and exterminate Christianity," and he bewails that "the Christian people are in the edge of a cliff."

The Ottoman historian Nashri states:

"It is narrated that Sultan Mehmed was generous and just, brave, intellectual and religious, friend to scholars and honorable. He used to bring intellectuals from around the world to Istanbul and give them a salary. Even if there was someone who was qualified in his art he used to bring him and give him *ulufa* (salary given each three months). No one who comes to him could be left deprived. He used to give dinar to the poor who he encountered while he walked around. All the poor people of Istanbul reached his support at some point. He was modest and far from pride. Even when he is in his grandness once he sees a dervish he acts with modesty. In his time scholars, righteous people, poets, and poor people were living in prosperity. If one would take another's dirham, he wouldn't even care about it. Thievery, adultery, and brigandage were over. If a woman traveled alone in a vehicle full of gold for two days, no one would bother or harm her."

Hodja Sadaddin Effendi emphasizes the nobility and grandness of his character:

"There wasn't an end to his good manner that should be praised nor to his attitude that should be applauded. He had such an understanding of justice that he wouldn't harm an ant for the country of Salomon. He never wanted to leave the oppressed face misfortune. He was so generous that the pen that would try to calculate his graces would get confused. He was such a sultan that Behram would be ashamed from his braveness, and İsfendiyar would be ashamed from his story. Wherever his flags points, victory festivals and happiness took over that country."

CONCLUSION

Fatih Sultan Mehmed realized a dream of various rulers by conquering Istanbul when he was twenty-one years old. When we consider him from this perspective, he had an exceptional personality. This extraordinary man who had determination and volition, who applied decisions unconditionally, was intolerant concerning governing the state, was also able to keep his calmness and sobriety, he was knowledgeable, he spoke various languages, and he was also a poet; he was compared to various emperors by the historians. Napoleon, Alexander, Cesar, and many others; certainly those great historical personalities have important merits. But few of them, maybe none of them, was as unique and versatile as Fatih: This ruler who is a fearless fighter on the battlefield, a smart tactician on the table, an intellectual in the classroom, a sentimental romantic with the pen in his hand, a man of action, a believer with a solid faith far from bigotry, doubtfully is one of the most interesting personalities of history.

Bravery and heroism were the most important sides of this sultan's personality. He rode his horse against the enemy, in order to realize the plans that he had in his mind and achieve his objectives. Determination and perseverance, volition and bravery were gathered in his spirit. After the discordance and the doubtfulness that occurred among the soldiers during the Siege of Belgrade, he rode his horse insanely on the enemy and he clashed with them; he killed three Serbian soldiers and was wounded on his forehead and his leg, the wound on forehead stayed for the rest of his life as a souvenir of Belgrade. He also dived into the enemy's army in the Expedition of Bogdan after the Janissaries lay down once they faced the defending system that was established by the voivode inside the forest and the cannons that he fired, and with this move he played a determining role in obtaining this victory. After Baltaoğlu was defeated in the naval warfare, which took place in Zeytinburnu against the Genoese galleons during the Siege of Istanbul, he rode his horse to the sea, as Hammer says, as if he wanted to take the victory from the Genoese.

Fatih, who was a man of struggle and action, participated in twenty-five expeditions during his life. He didn't share the information about the expeditions with anybody, so he aimed to catch his enemy unexpectedly and unprepared. He wanted to obtain the countries that he wanted to conquer without war, and he avoided damaging the economic structure of those countries. He would begin first by seizing a castle or a city.

He would calculate and analyze the expeditions and wars that he was planning with its details, and he would develop alternative plans according to the possible malfunctions. The best example for that is how he examined and studied the city walls, and after determining their strong and weak sides he planned the Siege of Istanbul, which he realized when he was only twenty-one years old. He constructed the Rumelian Castle in the best area to prevent supporting the city and powered it with cannons and also established his headquarters in front of Topkapı, which was one of the weakest points of the expedition. The fact that the Emperor Constantine established his headquarters in the same place in order to protect this weak area better and that the Ottoman soldiers entered the city from Topkapı proves how this estimation was correct. We have to remember also his move that drove the Byzantines into the corner and made them lose their motivation: He transported the boats on land with an unbelievable attempt and take them down to Haliç so he surrounded the Byzantines completely.

Fatih, who was a successful marshal and a brave character, was also an expert diplomat. We can see examples of that if we analyze his life: In the beginning of his sultanate, which means when he was only twenty years old, he accepted tolerantly the new demands of the Byzantine messengers, and hid his real aim in order to not frighten his enemy. Besides that he chose to ally with the Hungarians and the Italians in order to prevent a possible Crusade expedition. During the siege of Istanbul although he knew that the Galatians were helping the Byzantines he disregarded this situation in order to not expand the battlefield, but after the conquest he immediately transformed Galata into a Turkish land. During the expedition of Otlukbeli, he tolerated the Hungarian messengers in order to prevent any kind of support that might come from Europe; the messengers believed that they would get whatever they asked. At the same time the Venetian land was constantly attacked by the Janissaries in order to oppress it, and Venice could send help to Ak Koyunlu and Karamanlides only through the Mediterranean.

His military moves were never done randomly but rather they were aiming at a well-studied and planned objective. When we analyze the last years of his sultanate, we see that he realized all of his objectives in the Black Sea, Balkans, Aegean, and Anatolia. It was his turn to take Rome, and he started to work on it. But his lifetime wasn't enough for that.

Fatih Sultan Mehmed is a historical personage that everyone, including his friends and enemies, had to accept his talent and intelligence. He transformed the Ottoman state to a real empire and put the state on stable ground. Certainly the state and army system that was established by Fatih had great contributions in stopping the dangers coming from Europe.

We appreciate the value of what we have except when we lose it. It is enough to remember what Muslims have experienced after the First World War once the Ottoman Empire was dismissed from the history, in order to understand the importance of the Ottomans.

REFERENCES

Abdülkadir Özcan, "Akıncı Maddesi," *Türkiye Diyanet Vakfı İslam Ansiklopedisi*, vol. 2, İstanbul, 1989.

Abdülkadir Özcan, *Atam Dedem Kanunu Fatih Kanunnamesi*, Yitik Hazine, İstanbul, 2013.

A. Adnan Adıvar, *Osmanlı Türklerinde İlim*, Remzi Kitabevi, İstanbul, 2000.

Ahmet Şimşirgil, *Birincil Kaynaklardan Osmanlı Tarihi-Kayı*, vol 2, Şems Kitapları, İstanbul, 2006.

Ahmet Yaşar Ocak, "İstanbul'un Fethinin İdeolojik Arka Planı," *550. Yılında Fetih ve İstanbul Bildiriler*, TTK Yayınları, Ankara, 2007.

Ahmed bin Hanbel, *Müsned*, vol. 4, Ocak Yayıncılık, İstanbul, 2013.

Ali Sevim; Yaşar Yücel, *Klasik Dönemin Üç Hükümdarı: Fatih, Yavuz, Kanuni*, TTK Yayınları, Ankara, 1991.

Ali Sevim; Yaşar Yücel, *Türkiye Tarihi*, TTK Yayınları, Ankara, 1995.

Ali Yardım, "Fetih Hadisi Üzerinde Bir Araştırma," *Diyanet İşleri Başkanlığı Dergisi*, XIII/2 (Mart- Nisan Sayısı).

Alphonse de Lamartine, *Cihan Hâkimiyeti-Türkiye Tarihi*, vol. 3, Tercüman 1001 Temel Eser.

Cahid Baltacı, *XV. ve XVI. Yüzyıllarda Osmanlı Medreseleri*, Marmara Üniversitesi İlahiyat Vakfı Yayınları, İstanbul, 2005.

Carter V. Findley, *Dünya Tarihinde Türkler*, Kitap Yayınevi, İstanbul, 2008.

Daniel Goffman, *Osmanlı Dünyası ve Avrupa 1300–1700*, Kitap Yayınevi, İstanbul, 2008.

Ekmeleddin İhsanoğlu, "Eğitim ve Bilim," *Osmanlı Medeniyeti Tarihi*, vol. 2, Zaman Feza Yayıncılık, İstanbul, 1999.

Erendiz Özbayoğlu, "550. Yılında Fetih ve İstanbul," *Bildiriler*, TTK Yayınları, Ankara, 2007.

Ergeni Raduşev, "Balkanlar ve Fetih," 550. Yılında Fetih ve İstanbul," *Bildiriler*, TTK Yayınları, Ankara, 2007.

Feridun Emecen, *Osmanlı Klasik Çağında Savaş*, Timaş Yayınları, İstanbul, 2009.

Feridun Emecen, *İlk Osmanlılar ve Batı Anadolu Beylikler Dünyası*, Kitabevi Yayınları, İstanbul, 2005.

Feridun Emecen, "Osmanlı Siyasi Tarihi," *Osmanlı Devleti Tarihi*, vol. 1, Editör Ekmeleddin İhsanoğlu, Zaman Feza Yayıncılık, İstanbul, 1999.

Feridun Emecen, *Fetih ve Kıyamet*, Timaş Yayınları, İstanbul, 2012.

Franz Babinger, *Fatih Sultan Mehmed ve Zamanı*, Oğlak Yayınları, İstanbul, 2003.

Fuad Köprülü, *Osmanlı İmparatorluğu'nun Kuruluşu*, Akçağ Yayınları, Ankara, 2003.

Giacomo E. Carretto, *Akdeniz'de Türkler*, TTK Yayınları, Ankara, 2000.

H. Çetin Arslan, *Türk Akıncı Beyleri ve Balkanların İmarına Katkıları*, Kültür Bakanlığı Yayınları, Ankara, 2001.

Hakkı Dursun Yıldız, *Doğuştan Günümüze Büyük İslam Tarihi*, vol. 3, Çağ Yayınları, İstanbul, 1992.

Halil İnalcık, *Osmanlı İmparatorluğunun Klasik Çağı*, YKY, İstanbul.

Halil İnalcık, *Osmanlılar; Fütuhat, İmparatorluk, Avrupa ile İlişkiler*, Timaş Yayınları, İstanbul, 2010.

Halil İnalcık, *Kuruluş Dönemi Osmanlı Sultanları*, İsam Yayınları, İstanbul, 2010.

Halil İnalcık, *Fatih Devri Üzerinde Tetkikler ve Vesikalar*, TTK Yayınları, Ankara, 2007

Halil İnalcık, *Devlet-i Aliyye*, İş Bankası Kültür Yayınları, İstanbul, 2011.

Halil inalcık-Mevlüt Oğuz, *Gazavat-ı Sultan Murad B. Mehemmed Han*, TTK Basımevi, Ankara 1989.

Halil İnalcık,"Türk Devletlerinde Sivil Kanun Geleneği," *Türkiye Günlüğü Dergisi*, nr. 58, 1999.

Hüseyin Algül, *Büyük Fetih ve Sonrası*, Nil Yayınları, İzmir, 1991.

İbrahim Kafesoğlu, *Türk Milli Kültürü*, Boğaziçi Yayınları, İstanbul, 1993.

İlber Ortaylı, *Osmanlıyı Yeniden Keşfetmek*,Timaş Yayınları, İstanbul, 2009.

İlber Ortaylı, *Tarihimiz ve Biz*, Timaş Yayınları, İstanbul, 2009.

İlber Ortaylı-Taha Akyol, *Osmanlı Mirası*, Timaş Yayınları, İstanbul, 2010.

İsmail Hakkı Uzunçarşılı, *Osmanlı Devleti'nin İlmiye Teşkilatı*, TTK, Ankara, 1998.

İsmail Hakkı Uzunçarşılı, *Osmanlı Tarihi*, vol. 2, TTK Basımevi, Ankara, 1995.

İsmail Hakkı Uzunçarşılı, "Akıncı Maddesi," *İslam Ansiklopedisi*, vol. 1, 1940.

İsmet Miroğlu, "Fetret Devrinden II. Bayezide Kadar Osmanlı Siyasi Tarihi," *Doğuştan Günümüze Büyük İslam Tarihi Ansiklopedisi*, vol. 10, Çağ Yayınları, İstanbul, 1992.

Jean Paul Roux, *Türklerin Tarihi, Pasifikten Akdeniz'e 2000 Yıl*, Kabalcı Yayınevi, İstanbul, 2007.

Josefh von Hammer Burgstall, *Osmanlı Devleti Tarihi*, Üçdal Neşriyat, İstanbul, 1983.

Levon Panos Debağyan, *Paylaşılamayan Belde Konstantiniyye*, IQ Kültür Sanat Yayınları, İstanbul, 2003.

Machiavelli, *Hükümdar*, Göçebe Yayınları, İstanbul, 1997.

Mehmet Zeki Pakalın, *Osmanlı Tarih Deyimleri ve Terimleri Sözlüğü*, MEB Yayınları, İstanbul, 1966.

Mehmet Ali Ünal, *Osmanlı Müesseseleri Tarihi*, Isparta, 1997.

Mehmed Neşri, *Kitab-ı Cihannüma, Neşri Tarihi*, (eds.) Faik Reşit Unat, Mehmet Altay Köymen, TTK Basımevi, Ankara, 1987.

Mustafa Akdağ, *Türkiye'nin İktisadi ve İçtimai Tarihi*, Cem Yayınevi, İstanbul, 1995.

Mustafa Armağan, *Ufukların Sultanı, Fatih Sultan Mehmed*, Timaş Yayınları, İstanbul, 2010.

Necdet Sakaoğlu, *Bu Mülkün Sultanları*, Oğlak Yayınları, İstanbul, 1999.

Nicolas Vatin, "II. Bayezid'in Diplomasi Araçları," *Harp ve Sulh Osmanlılar*, (ed.) Dejanirah Couto, (tr.) Şirin Tekeli, Kitap Yayınevi, İstanbul, 2010.

Nicolae Jorga, *Osmanlı İmparatorluğu Tarihi*, Yeditepe Yayınları, İstanbul, 2009.

Nihal Atsız, *Âşık Paşaoğlu Tarihi*, MEB Yayınları, İstanbul, 1992.

Osman Turan, *Türk Cihan Hâkimiyeti Mefkûresi Tarihi*, Boğaziçi Yayınları, İstanbul, 1996.

Paul Wittek, "Devşirme ve Şeriat," *Türkiye Günlüğü Dergisi*, nr. 58, 1999.

Selahattin Tansel, *Osmanlı Kaynaklarına Göre Fatih Sultan Mehmed'in Siyasi ve Askeri Faaliyeti*, TTK Yayınları, Ankara, 1999.

Şehabettin Tekindağ, "Mahmut Paşa Maddesi," *TDV İslam Ansiklopedisi*, İstanbul, 1989.

Yılmaz Öztuna, *Büyük Osmanlı Tarihi*, Ötüken Neşriyat, İstanbul, 1994.